Make Your Own Animated Movies and Videotapes

Make Your Own Animated Movies and Videotapes

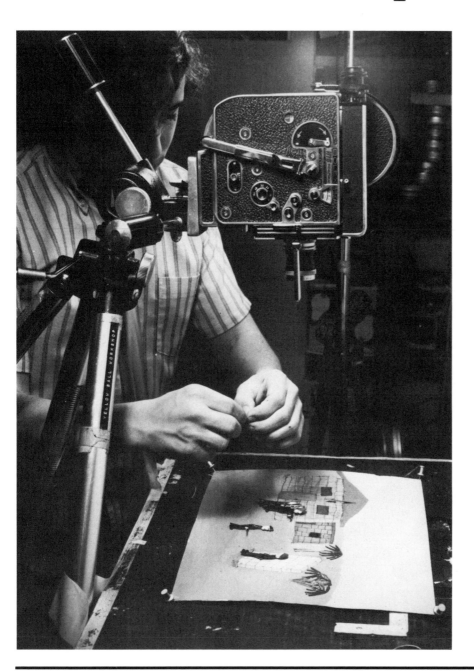

Film and Video Techniques from the Yellow Ball Workshop

by Yvonne Andersen

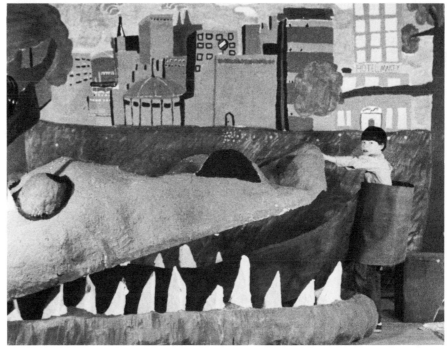

Little, Brown and Company
Boston Toronto London

This book is dedicated to Bruce Bolduc,
a former student and an esteemed colleague,
who would have liked to see it finished.

This book is an updated and expanded edition of Yvonne Andersen's
Make Your Own Animated Movies: Yellow Ball Workshop Film Techniques,
which was published by Little, Brown and Company in 1970.

Library of Congress Cataloging-in-Publication Data

Andersen, Yvonne.
    Make your own animated movies and videotapes / by Yvonne Andersen.
        p.   cm.
    Updated, expanded ed. of: Make your own animated movies. 1st ed.
1970.
    Summary: Instructions for making animated movies including drawing
the cartoon, operating the camera, and synchronizing the sound. Also
describes the equipment needed.
    ISBN 0-316-03941-1
    1. Animation (Cinematography) — Juvenile literature.
    [1. Cinematography.   2. Animation (Cinematography)   3. Amateur
motion pictures.]   I. Andersen, Yvonne.   Make your own animated
movies.   II. Title.
    TR897.5.A53   1991
    778.5'247 — dc20   90-33756

10 9 8 7 6 5 4 3 2 1

HAL

Published simultaneously in Canada by Little, Brown & Company
(Canada) Limited

PRINTED IN THE UNITED STATES OF AMERICA

Dear Reader,

My last two books on animation were published in 1970. Since then our students at the Yellow Ball Workshop have created some wonderful projects. These films are in distribution, and available for people to see, but I also want to share the adventure of making them, and to describe the many new techniques developed in the last two decades.

The Yellow Ball Workshop gave its first courses in film animation for children in 1963. In the past twenty-six years, we at the workshop have been concerned with several things: how to bring to life on the screen the fantastical, bizarre, and mysterious images of children's art; how best to communicate these strange and interesting stories and sounds; how to get the best results with the least work and expense; how to make sure that we all have a good time learning the techniques and making the art; how to find animation techniques that don't require extensive drawing skills; and how to make high-quality work on generally available equipment.

In this book I describe some of our experiences with different animation techniques, equipment, and media, including super-8mm and 16mm film, videotape, and computers.

This book is made for children ages ten and up, teachers, and beginning animators of all ages. Animation — whether on film, videotape, or computer — is becoming more important not only in the areas of entertainment and artistic expression, but also in education, where it is used to explain math and science, and in commerce, where it is used to teach pilots how to fly and to help designers build cities.

We think that this book will be of interest to those who recognize this increasing role and who consider film, video, and computer animation to be one of the most popular and important art forms of the twentieth century.

Yvonne Andersen

Yellow Ball Workshop
LEXINGTON, MASSACHUSETTS

Acknowledgments

I would like to thank Robert Vennerbeck, Dennis Hlynsky, David Fain, and Michael DiGregorio for their assistance with video and computer animation projects. I am grateful to Albert Hurwitz, who was director of the Newton Creative Arts Center during the fifteen-year period when some of these projects were created.

Thanks also go to Peter O'Neill, Amy Kravitz, David Porter, and the faculty and staff of the Film/Video Department of the Rhode Island School of Design; to John Culkin, director of the Center for Understanding Media, which was responsible for many film education projects in public schools throughout the country; to Cynthia Stone, Department of Education, Museum of Fine Arts, Boston; and to Judith Woodruff, director of International Arts for Peace.

Much credit is due my students and assistants, including my children, Paul Falcone and Jean Falcone, at the Yellow Ball Workshop during twenty-six years of animation projects and classes.

And I greatly appreciate the contribution of Dominic Falcone, my husband, who has helped with everything.

Make Your Own Animated Movies and Videotapes

Contents

Three-dimensional Animation 89

1   Making a Movie without a Camera

Did you know that you can make animated movies without a camera? You can do this by drawing your images directly onto movie film. You may draw on super-8mm, 16mm, or 35mm film. It is amazing that such tiny pictures can be projected twenty feet wide in a movie theater!

When a movie is shown, one picture (*frame*) is projected onto the screen at a time. 16mm film runs through the projector at the rate of twenty-four of these tiny frames per second. It doesn't matter if they are live-action frames (with live actors) or animated frames (with drawn characters).

The frames are projected so fast the human eye doesn't notice that they are separate pictures, each one just a little different from the one before it. They just seem to blend together to create the illusion of action. This is called *persistence of vision*. If you make twenty-four separate drawings on twenty-four consecutive frames of film, your movie will last for one second on the screen.

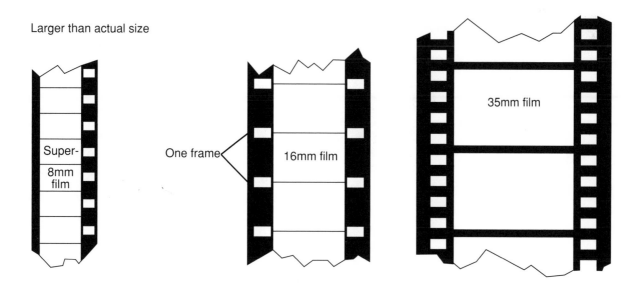

Larger than actual size

Super-8mm film

One frame

16mm film

35mm film

Let's say you want a simple image, such as a dot, to appear on the screen for one second. If you are working in 16mm, you will have to draw that dot twenty-four times, or once on each of twenty-four frames. The opposite page illustrates one-third second of film showing a dot getting larger until it fills the whole page.

Drawing on Film

To begin, tape down some clean, white paper on your worktable. Then, sit down and *spool off* (roll off) about six feet of *clear leader* (the type of film you need for drawing) vertically, *emulsion* (dull) side up, in front of you, onto the table. This will be used later, to thread the projector.

If you are using a hundred-foot reel of film, hold that feed reel in your lap, or fasten it under the edge of your table with tape, so you can spool film off it. The portion you work with must be on the table. As you finish your drawings, feed the film forward across the table, away from you.

Using a thin-tipped felt marker or crow-quill pen point, draw on the emulsion side of the film. (Your color might not stick on the *base* [shiny] side of the film.)

Film leader does not have any frame lines on it to show you what area will be projected onto the screen. In the drawings below, the frame is the area of the film between the holes, or *perforations*, as indicated by dotted lines.

Correct   Incorrect

Do not draw these lines on the film, but remember where the frame is when you make your drawings. If you do not center the drawings, your finished movie will appear on the screen as an abstract image, rather than the image you planned. (It is OK to draw in the area outside the frame, between the perforations, but that part will not be projected. This has been done in the abstract example on the opposite page.)

Remember to spool off three feet of clear leader, for the *tail leader*, after you finish your project.

If you are working in super 8mm, the projector can be run at the rate of eighteen frames per second instead of twenty-four. In this case you would draw eighteen dots to get one second of film, or nine dots for one-half second.

If you are in a classroom with a lot of animators working on the same hundred-foot reel of film, it is easier to tape the film down horizontally, separating each animator's three-foot section from his or her neighbors' sections with pieces of masking tape.

Each animator turns to the left and works from the left end of the film to the right (see the drawing below).

When everyone is finished, remove the tape and rewind the film so it can be projected.

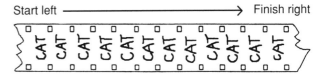

The film can be run forward and backward, until everyone has seen it several times. Fast classical or popular music (played from a record, audiotape, or compact disc) would probably go well with this kind of project.

Scratching on Film

In *The Cosmic Crystal*, a film made by one student at the Yellow Ball Workshop, a female alien stuns her enemy with an electric beam that comes from two spots on her forehead. This beam was created by scratching on the film.

For accurate scratching and drawing of images on film, use a small magnifying glass on a stand. The least expensive scratching tool is an aluminum pushpin.

You can also scratch the emulsion surface of *black leader*. In this technique black emulsion comes off, leaving a clear area, which is projected as white. This clear area can also be colored with permanent markers. The black emulsion scratches off more easily when it has first been moistened slightly with a damp cloth.

After you have completed your scratching, be sure to clean the film with velvet or Vebril Wipes (cloth pads) to remove the scraps of loose film. Don't use liquid film cleaner in drawing-on-film projects.

You can thread your projector with a length of film, and then splice the ends together, creating a *loop*. Be sure the film is threaded so it will run over both the feed reel and the *take-up reel*. This loop of film can be run continuously.

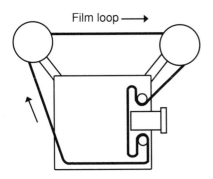

Film loop ⟶

IMPORTANT: NEVER DRAW OR SCRATCH DIRECTLY ON VIDEOTAPE. IT WILL RUIN BOTH THE TAPE AND YOUR VCR!

Cleanup

It is important to clean out the *gate* of the projector after you have finished projecting a drawing-on-film or scratching-on-film project. There may be tiny pieces of film, emulsion, or ink left in the gate, and these can scratch movies run later on the same projector. For cleaning you may use cotton swabs moistened with *denatured alcohol*, or a small brush that usually comes with the projector. Always clean out the gate of any projector before showing a movie, in order to prevent scratches on the film.

Film and Art Supplies and Equipment

Film

Super-8mm white leader is the cheapest, but the drawing area is the smallest. It can be bought in fifty-foot lengths from camera stores.

16mm clear leader is easier to draw on, as the area is larger. A hundred-foot reel of double-perforated 16mm clear leader with an emulsion, or black, leader may be ordered from Eastman Kodak or from motion picture laboratories where 16mm film is developed. Most large cities have such labs, so this is the most convenient format to use.

35mm film gives you a bigger drawing area but is much more expensive. The clear leader must be ordered from a motion picture lab. Unless you have access to a 35mm commercial movie theater projector, you will need to send your 35mm drawing-on-film project to a motion picture lab for copying onto super-8mm or 16mm film.

Art Supplies

Markers: Staedtler Lumocolor S313 permanent thin-tip markers in eight colors. If you have purchased clear leader *with an emulsion* (slightly more expensive), you can draw on the emulsion side with less expensive, water-soluble markers such as Big Sig. These can be purchased in art supply stores.

Inks: Pelican T for Plastic Sheets is used with tiny watercolor brushes or crow-quill pen points in penholders. This gives more texture, but the inks take twenty minutes to dry and require a more careful cleaning of the gate after projection.

Equipment

Super-8mm projectors and viewers can be rented if you don't own them.

16mm projectors: Most public schools have 16mm projectors, and some public libraries lend them. New and used 16mm projectors are available from camera stores and equipment rental houses.

2   Equipment for Making a Movie with a Camera

Cameras

You can use several kinds of cameras when making your own animated movies — a super-8mm or 16mm film camera, or a video camcorder, which can take just a few frames at a time.

Pictured here are three types of cameras used at the Yellow Ball Workshop.

Bolex 16mm camera

Nizo super-8mm camera

Sony Video 8 Pro CCD-V220 camcorder

Close-up Diopters

Your work will be much easier if you have a set of close-up *diopters* for your film or video camera. These additional lenses are screwed onto the front of the camera lens. They will let you film a wide area of artwork with the camera about eighteen inches away. They will also let you *zoom* the camera in and out at this range.

Close-up diopters usually come in sets of three: +1, +2, and +3. The most valuable of them is the +1 diopter, which lets you position the camera about twenty-four inches away from the artwork. Plus 2 lets you move closer, about eighteen inches away, and +3 about twelve inches.

When buying close-up diopters take your camera to the store to make sure that they can screw onto your lens. Sometimes it's necessary to buy an adapter ring in order to attach the diopters to your lens. If they are just a little big, you can tape them to the lens with black masking tape.

If you don't have diopters, you must be from three to six feet away from the artwork. This is all right for three-dimensional sets and characters, but inconvenient for flip books and cutouts.

Many cameras have *macro*, or close-up, capability built into them. This is fine, but it does not take the place of close-up diopters, as you cannot zoom in and out in the macro setting, and your artwork must be tiny.

Cable Release

Super-8mm cameras need a *cable release* in order to take single frames. Take your camera to the camera store so you can be sure to buy a release that fits. Look for one that has the largest possible head on it, as your thumb will be pressing it frequently.

With Bolex 16mm cameras, cable releases are not necessary. If the camera is on a firm tripod, you can press the frame release forward carefully enough that the camera will not jiggle.

The Sony Video 8 Pro CCD-V220 camcorder takes as few as eight frames at a time if you slide forward the red button marked RECORD on the VTR panel. However, the RM-84 Remote Commander, an accessory remote control, is more convenient for this purpose.

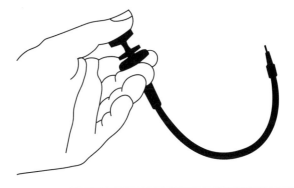

Tripod or Animation Stand

The most useful support for beginning animators is a *tripod*. We at the Yellow Ball Workshop recommend that you purchase a sturdy one, which will cost about $150. Such a tripod will hold a super-8mm, 16mm, or video-8 camera steady. It can hold the camera in a vertical position for flat animation, or in a horizontal position for three-dimensional sets and live-action filming.

Filming Table

A small, low children's table is a useful type of support for artwork in flat animation. Three-dimensional sets can be put on a regular kitchen table or worktable.

Lights

For flat animation, we use two Acme Flyweight stands and deep Acme-Lite ten-inch reflectors with 250-watt bulbs of 3200K (3200 degrees Kelvin) color temperature.

Tape the two front legs of the tripod to the legs of the table with *duct tape*. Tape the rear leg of the tripod to the floor.

Super-8mm Film

The best super-8mm film for animation is Kodachrome 40. Higher quality copies can be made from it. Since it has a low light sensitivity, or *ASA rating,* of 40 under artificial light, you will need plenty of light when using this film. Kodachrome 40 is fine for flat animation if you use two 250-watt light bulbs of 3200K. It's also good for filming live action outdoors on a sunny day.

You might need to use Ektachrome 160, which has an ASA of 160, for three-dimensional sets, as they tend to need more light. This film can also be used outdoors on a cloudy day.

Both Kodachrome 40 and Ektachrome 160 require seven to ten days for processing, as they must be sent to Kodak. If you are in a hurry, you can use a slightly lower quality film called Ektachrome 7244, which has an ASA of 160 and can be processed locally.

Lights can be omitted entirely, if you set up flat animation next to a large window, but you cannot do this with three-dimensional sets, because there will not be enough light.

A useful lighting arrangement for small sets includes five Smith Victor S-8-4 light stands with PL-8 orange reflectors and *barn doors*, and one Smith Victor *boom.*

A boom is a stand that holds a long metal rod, which extends over the set and holds a separate light on the end. It can be raised, lowered, and pointed in any direction. You can rig up something homemade for this purpose.

Barn doors are shields fastened to a reflector to direct the light. You can close them to allow less light, or open them for more.

As mentioned 3200K is the correct color temperature for the Kodachrome or Ektachrome film. Don't try to put these 250- or 500-watt bulbs in cheap reflectors from a hardware store, which are not built to take such high wattage.

Most super-8mm color films are meant to be used indoors, with artificial light. Set the filter of your camera for indoor use with these films.

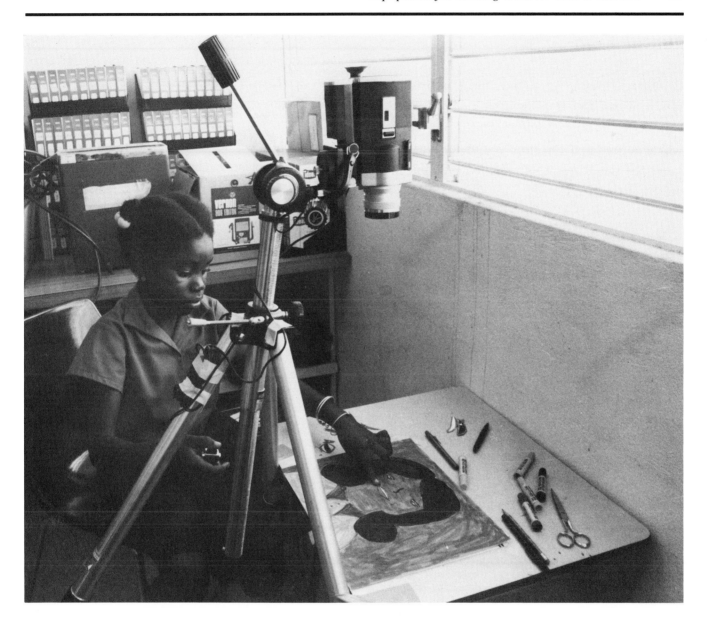

16mm Film

If you are filming in 16mm, the least expensive film you can use is a hundred-foot roll of Ektachrome 7240 (tungsten) film. This is *reversal* film, which means that the film you shoot with is the same one that (after it's developed) you put in the projector to screen.

If you can't get Ektachrome 7240, you can use *negative* film. This ends up being a little more expensive, as the laboratory must first develop this negative, and then make a *positive*, or reversal, print for you to project.

Negatives, which are very sensitive to scratching and dust, should never be opened or screened after processing, except by the lab when it is making another copy.

Negative film has some advantages, though. If you scratch your print, a new, scratch-free print can be made from your negative by the lab. Lighting mistakes made with negative film are more easily corrected by the lab.

Bolex 16mm cameras use removable lenses. We like to use the Pan Cinor 17mm-to-85mm zoom lens with these cameras.

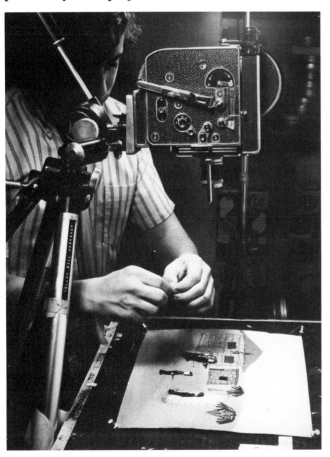

You can also use a 10mm or a 16mm lens that doesn't zoom. The camera in this scene has a 10mm lens.

Light Meters

If you are using a Bolex camera, you need a separate light meter. We use a Gossen Luna Pro with a *repro attachment.* To take a reading, place the artwork so it faces the camera and the lights. Then, lay the meter on the artwork, and measure your reading from the green pointer. Set the meter to match the reading.

When filming three-dimensional sets, remove the repro attachment. Prop up a *gray card* against the puppets, and point your light meter at the card, taking the reading from the yellow pointer on the meter.

Repro attachment

Gossen Luna Pro light meter

Video-8 Camcorder

Camcorder means that both the *cam*era (which takes the pictures) and the tape re*corder* deck (which records the images and sound) are in one piece of equipment. The earlier cameras and decks were two separate components that had to be used together to shoot a videotape.

Video 8 is a new format for videotape. The tape comes in a tiny cassette the size of an audiocassette.

Thirty-minute video-8 cassette

Video equipment that can record one frame at a time is fairly expensive. Manufacturers have not yet produced inexpensive video camcorders that can do this. Sony has come up with the excellent Video 8 Pro CCD-V220 camcorder, which can take eight frames at a time without any *glitches* between groups of eight frames. (Glitches look like snow between shots.)

Most animators shoot in groups of two or three frames. Groups of eight will certainly give you animation, but it will not move smoothly. However, it would be good practice to prepare scenes and shoot in eights until you have access to a film camera.

Some MTV-type animation looks good when shot in eight-frame segments. Your story, artwork, and timing can be designed for that type of animation.

One video filming technique that will allow you to shoot in groups of four frames is described on page 39. You can also shoot in eights, or even short bursts of twenty-four or more, and then edit each group down to three or four frames on a video editing console.

Schools and animators with larger budgets can purchase a color video animation stand called Video Pencil Test Systems. This equipment will take one frame at a time, and is available from Animation Controls, Inc., in Vista, California.

Film equipment has been around for many years, and is still being used. Video equipment is newer, and it is changing rapidly. We expect that the single-frame video camera will eventually come down low enough in price to be found in many homes.

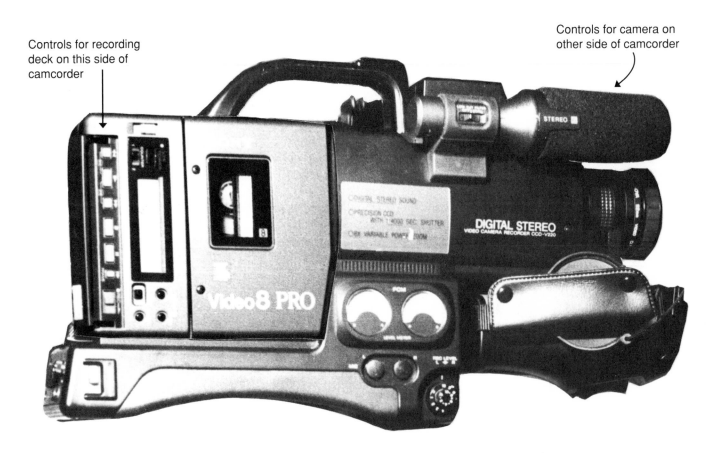

Controls for camera on other side of camcorder

Controls for recording deck on this side of camcorder

Flat Animation

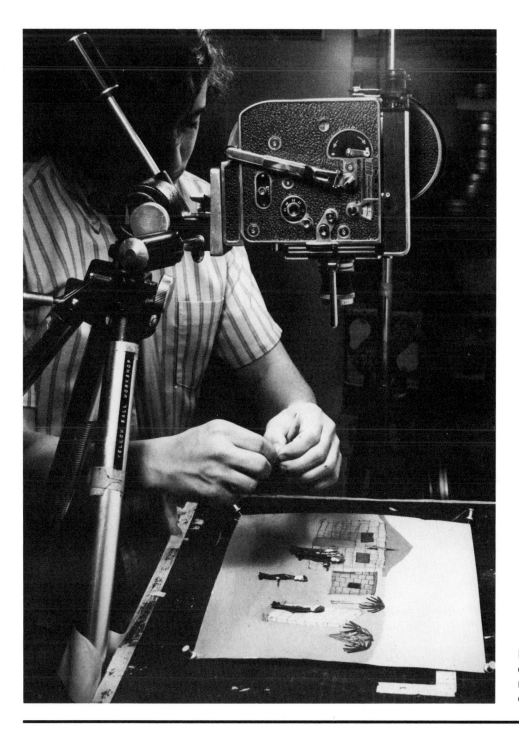

Flat animation uses drawings, paintings, and materials that don't stick out from the surface.

3　Flip Books

Flip books are collections of small drawings bound together in book form. Each drawing is just a little different from the one before it. When you flip the pages through your fingers, the drawings appear to move. You can also shoot flip books to make film animation.

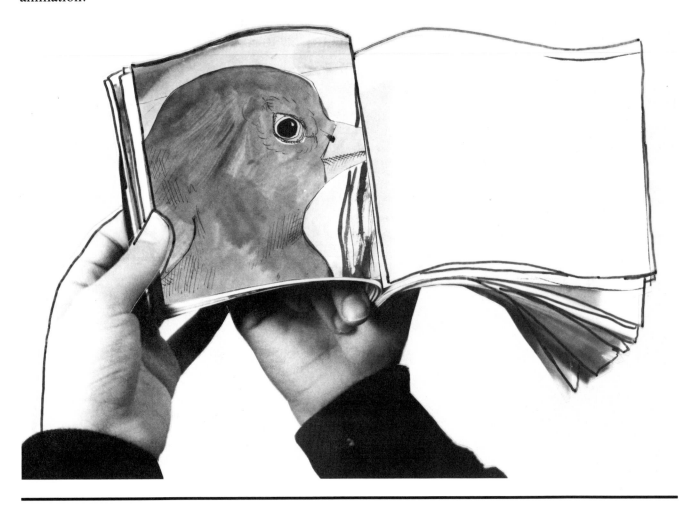

Preparing the Artwork

Begin with a *scratch pad* — a small pad of inexpensive white paper that you can buy from a stationery store. Scratch pads are about 4 by 6 inches, which is just a little too wide to be filmed (wrong ratio). Cut one-half inch off the end with a matte knife, making the pad 4 by 5½ inches.

Draw with the pad in a horizontal position. Start your drawings at the back of the pad, working with a black ballpoint pen. As the paper is thin enough to see through, you will be able to regulate the movement of your drawings. Each drawing should differ just a little from the last one. Number each drawing in the corner.

Try to keep the important part of the action in the middle. This is because the camera may or may not film the edges.

The area inside the dotted line is the only area that you can be sure will film. The rest may or may not film, but you should still paint all the way out to the edge of the paper.

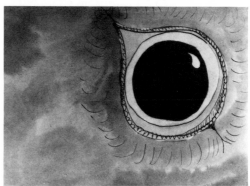

Film is projected at the rate of twenty-four frames (pictures) per second. Some animators film each drawing twice. For this, twelve drawings would be needed to make a one-second movie.

If you film each drawing three times you only need to make eight different drawings to make a one-second movie.

In the scene at the left, we need to see the weight lifter standing in place for at least one second before the action starts.

For this, the first drawing was traced to make two nearly identical versions. These were each filmed for three frames in alternation, until twenty-four frames, or one second, had elapsed.

The last drawing was done the same way as the first. The drawings in between were filmed for three frames each. This scene lasts 2½ seconds.

Flip books tend to have a lively, vibrating quality. If the first and last drawings, which were each used for a *hold*, had not been copied, part of the film would be missing that vibrating quality.

Cycles

The character doing push-ups can be filmed as a *cycle*.

This means the six drawings can be filmed over and over to make the action repeat.

In the film on the opposite page, the cycle was repeated four times for four push-ups, with the sounds ''grunt, groan'' on the sound track.

Titles

The title page shows the name of the film in large, readable letters positioned in the middle.

Shoot twenty-four frames for each major word in a title. Shoot an extra twenty-four just for the page. For example, when filming ''THE TREE,'' shoot a total of seventy-two frames.

Your name should be on the second page, and it is important to have a page that says, ''The End'' or ''Stop!'' This lets the audience know that the film is over, and that it's time to clap.

You could shoot the body of the film in threes, or in groups of any other number you wish. Ones will make the action move very fast, and you will have a short film. Sixes will slow it down, give it a sort of rhythm or beat, and make it a much longer film.

Complicated drawings take longer to ''read,'' and so should be filmed longer.

THE TREE

BY
BETTY
BROWN

THE
END

Setting Up the Camera

You can use the same camera setup for super 8mm, 16mm, or video 8.

Brace a small, low table against a wall. Brace the two front legs of the tripod against the front of the table.

These two front legs will be almost vertical. They will extend under the table a little. Anchor them to the table legs with duct tape.

Tape the rear leg of the tripod, which will extend backward, to the floor or rug. Fasten the camera to the tripod head, and point it vertically, down at the artwork.

Filming Flip Books

1. Load the film or videotape into the camera, and screw the +1 close-up diopter onto the camera lens.

2. Set the indoor or outdoor light filter on the camera.

3. Fasten the single-frame cable release onto the camera.

4. Point the camera vertically, down at the artwork on the table.

5. Adjust the camera lens so it is roughly eighteen inches from the artwork.

6. Set a light on each side of the filming table to light the artwork evenly.

7. Zoom the lens all the way in to the extreme *telephoto*, or close-up, position.

8. If you are using a video camera, set the focus to MANUAL.

9. Place printed letters on top of the artwork. If you can't focus on these letters, move the camera higher or lower on the tripod until they come into focus.

10. Zoom the lens out to your filming position.

11. If using a film camera, set it to record an area smaller than the whole artwork, because most cameras take a little more on all four sides than what you can see through the eyepiece.

12. Turn to the cardboard backing at the rear of the flip book. Across the top and bottom, draw a line one-quarter inch from the edge, and another one three-eighths inch from the edge. Along the right and left sides, draw a line one-half inch from the edge, and another one three-eighths inch from the edge.

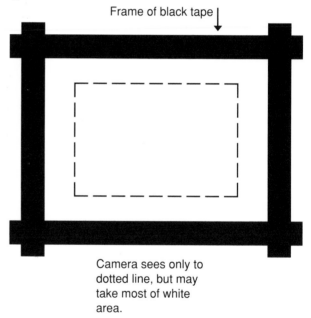

Frame of black tape

Camera sees only to dotted line, but may take most of white area.

13. Tape the cardboard backing to the table. The artwork and filming starts in the back. If the paper is thin enough so you can see the previous drawing through it, stick a spare blank page under each drawing before you film it.

14. Set up the camera to see the inside lines but not the outside ones. You don't have to do this with video cameras because they take just what you see through the eyepiece.

The thickness of the book will not interfere with your focusing the artwork, as the area of focus, or *depth of field*, is several inches deep.

In flip books with loose pages, each page is numbered in the corner. When you film this kind of flip book, first tape down a frame using black masking tape to show you where the drawings should be positioned. This positioning is called *registration*.

Film Ratios

If you wish to make your artwork larger than 4 by 5½ inches, be sure you keep the right *ratio* (correct relationship between the width and the height of the paper). Your picture must be in a horizontal format no matter what size it is. That is because the camera will film vertical artwork with extra space at sides.

If you wish to film artwork roughly the size of half a piece of typing paper, hold it horizontally and look at it through a camera lens. Zoom in and focus. Zoom out until you can just see the top and bottom edges of the paper.

Looking through the eyepiece, draw a line on the left and the right side of the paper where the other two edges should be. Cut off the extra paper outside these lines. This is now the correct ratio.

Field Guides

Some animators use a *field guide* to determine ratio. This is a clear, stiff sheet of plastic with registration holes in the bottom, and with all possible field ratios marked on it.

The twelve-field Acme punched field guide shows areas ranging from one to twelve fields. It may be placed over your artwork to see if it is the right ratio.

You can use a white plastic Acme *peg bar* for registration. The holes in the bottom of the field guide fit the pegs, holding punched animation *cels* or bond paper in registration with each other. A cel is a transparent sheet of acetate with registration holes at the bottom. You can draw and paint on it.

You can use either an Acme or an Oxberry field guide. They have different shaped holes, so you must always use the same type.

If you want to draw large animation, it is convenient to purchase twelve-field white bond paper prepunched for Acme registration, and an Acme peg bar.

Tape the peg bar near the edge of the table that is against the tripod. The holes in the paper will fit over the pegs on the bar, giving you very accurate registration.

The field guide, peg bar, animation bond paper, and animation cels can be bought from an animation supply house such as the Cartoon Color Company in Culver City, California.

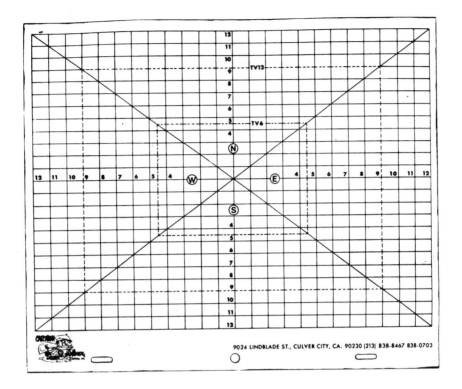

Twelve-field Acme punched field guide

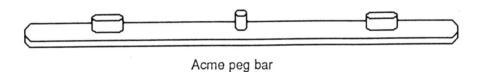

Acme peg bar

A *two-field* size measures
two squares in all directions
from the center.

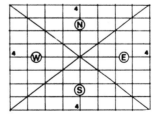

A *four-field* size measures
four squares in all directions
from the center.

Light Box

Some animators use a *light box* under their drawings, so that they can see their last drawing through the blank sheet on top of it as they make the next drawing. The light shining through the drawings will help you to estimate the changes needed.

A light box can also be used to help determine the correct ratio of your artwork. Turn on the light box and place the field guide on top of it. Then, place the artwork on top of the field guide. The lines of the field guide will show through the artwork. You can trace onto the artwork the four ratio lines that show the size you need.

The one we use looks like this. We made a triangular brace of slatted metal strips. Then we cut a hole in a piece of plywood, and taped the wood onto the brace. Underneath we placed a reflector holding a 75-watt light. We taped a piece of translucent white plastic on top of the hole.

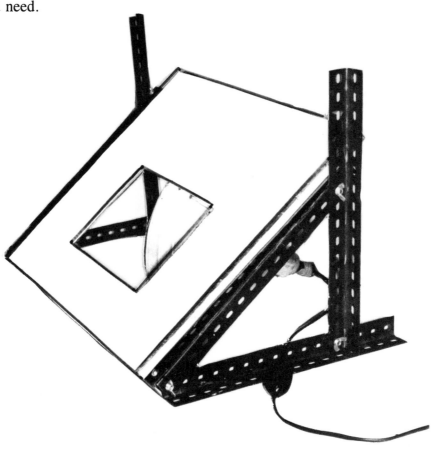

Filming Flip Books in Video 8

The basic animation setup for video cameras is exactly the same as for super-8mm film cameras. Turn on the camera section, and the VTR (video tape recorder), or recording deck section of the camcorder. After you have focused the camera, it will choose the proper light setting.

After you turn on the camera and the VTR, slide the red RECORD switch on the VTR panel to the side once to get ready. After this, every time you slide this switch, the camera will take eight frames. Be sure to wait for the camera to stop making its little noise *before* you take the next eight frames.

You may prefer to use the RECORD button on the accessory Remote Commander unit, which plugs into the back of the Sony Video 8 camcorder.

There is another way of shooting in video 8, which will cut down the number of frames taken each time from eight to four. This method is tedious and probably more wearing on the camera if done over a long period of time. Here is the formula:

1. **Press the red RECORD button three times.** This will record roughly twenty-four frames. Wait for the two whirring sounds to stop after each press.

2. **Press STOP once.** The cassette will rewind and erase about twenty frames, leaving four frames not erased.

3. **Press RECORD once more** to get ready to start again.

4. **Change your artwork to the next drawing.**

5. **Repeat** steps one through four.

This technique requires much more work, but videotape does have some advantages. You don't have to take the film to the lab, pay for it to be developed, or wait for its return.

4 Cutouts

Cutout animation is a fun technique for a beginning animator. You can get more results for less work than with most other techniques.

A cutout scene requires only one background drawing. The characters are separate, hinged paper dolls that move against that background.

First you tape the scenery paper to a tabletop. Then you carefully move the characters a little at a time.

Cutouts are usually filmed in twos. A walking man might move forward about one-quarter inch every two frames, a running man one-half inch or more.

When a character walks, the left arm moves forward together with the right leg, and the right arm with the left leg.

The speed of the movement depends on how many frames you take per movement, and how big a distance the character moves. The quality of the animation depends on how well you move the characters.

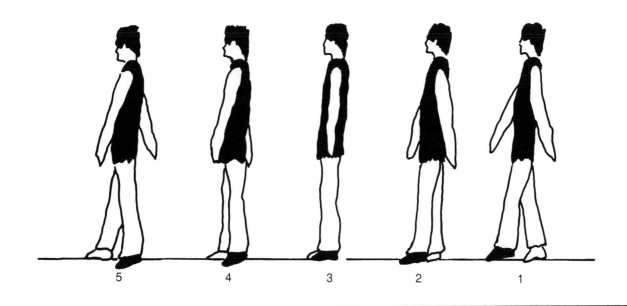

5　　　　　4　　　　　3　　　　　2　　　　　1

Four Basic Types of Scenes

There are four basic elements needed to make a short cutout animated film. These include *titles*, the *long shot*, the *medium shot*, and the *close-up*. All four should be in your first cutout film.

We have a special way of starting such a short film. You make the artwork first and the story later. Assemble paper, markers, paint or inks, scissors, pencil, and/or whatever other art supplies you like to work with.

First you will need to consider the size of the paper. Movie cameras take a *rectangular* picture that is wider than it is high, or horizontal. Here are some sizes or ratios you can use.

Cut this shape out of your paper. We prefer a heavy (two-ply), medium-finish *bristol board* for this work. Pads or separate sheets of this paper can be bought in art supply stores.

Bristol board is stiffer and stronger and will lie flatter after painting than something like typing paper. Medium-finish (nonslick) will absorb ink or paint best, but any kind of paper can be used.

8" high

11" wide

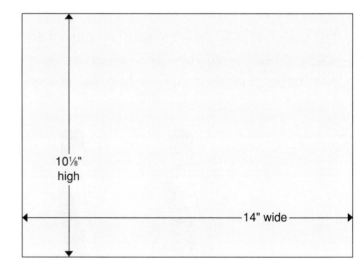

10⅛" high

14" wide

Titles

Include three main sections: the name of the film, your name and the names of others who helped, and the end title.

Medium Shot

Shows the main character from the waist up, or shows something else in a similar amount of space. Focuses on the action or the event that makes the film a story.

Long Shot

The place where the event is happening. This shot is like a landscape. It may also show people or creatures from head to toe.

Close-up

Shows the faces of the characters, or focuses attention on an important action.

Close-ups

The first step of this project is to create the close-up face of the character. Since this is a close-up, make the head large, leaving some space above it at the top of the page. Draw the shoulders all the way to the bottom of the page. Paint in the eyes and eyebrows, but not the eyeballs. Paint eyeballs on a separate sheet of paper and cut them out.

Don't paint the mouth on the face. Paint three (or more) different sizes of mouths on a separate sheet of paper — one mouth closed, the second partly open, the third wide open. Make the open mouths dark inside, and show some teeth in some of the mouths. Cut out these mouths, and see if they fit well on the face. If not, make another set, smaller or larger as needed.

If you decide to paint a small, closed mouth directly onto the face, you must make the other, cut-out mouths larger, so they will cover it when you animate.

Sketch in a simple background, or paint it a plain color. Don't make it complicated, because you want viewers to concentrate on the face in this scene. If the face is light in color, make the background darker so it will stand out. If the face is dark, make the background lighter.

Here the filmmaker decided to make extra mouths, and to cut out the head, so it could be moved on the background.

You will need to paint the background all the way to the edges of the paper because the camera may or may not film that far.

Scenes can be filmed out of sequence, and later edited into the right order.

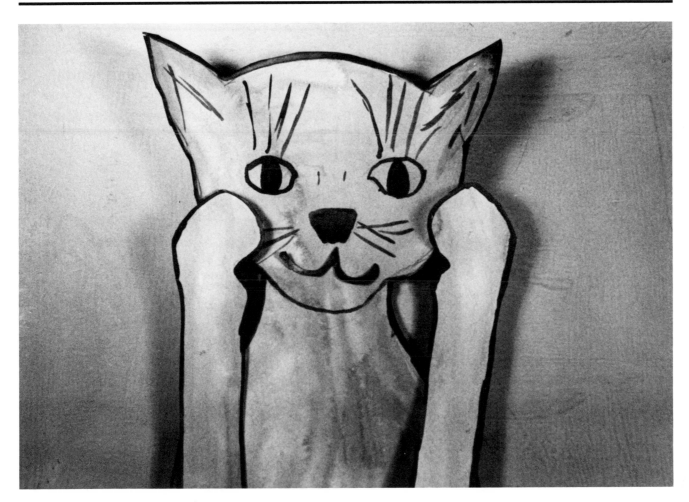

This cat is a cutout separate from the background, so it can move a little. The arms are separate from the body and can move into the scene. The head can also be cut loose from the body, so it can nod from side to side, and can be replaced by a head looking sideways.

Notice that there seems to be a shadow on the background. Shadows are the enemy of cutout animation. Most of the time you don't want them. If this background were a blue sky, the illusion would be ruined.

Ways to Get Rid of Shadows

1. Bend the head and paws down to make them lie flat.
2. If thin paper wrinkles, place it under a book overnight to flatten it.
3. Fold small pieces of masking tape over onto themselves to form loops. Place the loops under the ears and body of the cat, pressing them to the background.
4. Use a sheet of nonglare glass on top of the artwork. This usually eliminates all shadow problems.

The hand on the stick shift of the racing car above is separate from the stem of the shift.

Thread taped to the underside of the hand runs through a small hole punched at the top of the stem.

You can make such a hole with a pushpin. Tape the thread down tightly on the underside of the stem.

Using the thread you can make smooth circular or up-and-down hand movements.

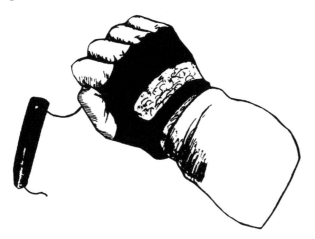

Long Shots

The second scene made is usually a long shot. This shows the full bodies of the characters. Since the face is small in the scene, paint but don't animate it. Hinge the arms and legs to the body so the character can walk.

Sketch the body parts of the characters lightly with a pencil, or paint them with poster paint, inks, or felt markers, and then cut them out.

Make the arms and legs a little longer at the hips and shoulders than you might expect. This is because you will slide them up slightly under the torso for hinging.

Don't try to draw a complete character in one piece and then cut it apart for hinging. The arms and legs will be too short.

If the size of your background is ten inches high and fourteen inches wide, the cutout character should be about five to seven inches tall.

Hinging

Hinges are made on the underside of the character with masking tape and thin sewing thread.

This flexible thread allows you to move the joints in any direction. A thicker thread or a plastic thread would cause the limbs to snap back into their original position, rather than stay where you want them.

If you are a beginning animator, hinge your figure only at the shoulders and hips. Always round the edges of the limbs slightly so that if an edge sticks out, it doesn't look strange.

Carefully hinged arms and legs are easy to animate.

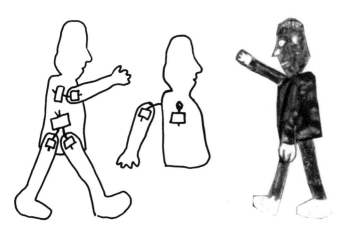

Hinge a human figure wearing a shirt and trousers by having the shirt outside the trousers or by thickening the legs at the upper thigh as they go under a belt.

There are two types of hinges. The *plain hinge* is shown on this page. You must always place the masking tape close to the end of the limb. Make the hinge tight.

A sideways character needs a *hole-punching hinge* at the shoulders. Imagine a circle near the end of the underside of the arm near the shoulder. Make a dot with a pencil in the center of that circle.

Then, lay the arm on the body, and estimate the spot where that dot is touching the body. Make a small hole at that spot *in the body only* with a pushpin.

Tape a piece of thread on the underside of the arm so the thread extends out from the dot. Pull the thread through the hole in the body, and tape it down tightly on the underside of the body.

Advanced animators also hinge characters at the elbows and knees. The hole-punching hinge is used for this purpose.

If your hole isn't in quite the right place, just take the joint apart and make another small hole. The incorrect hole will probably still be hidden by the arm.

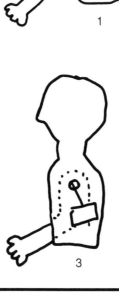

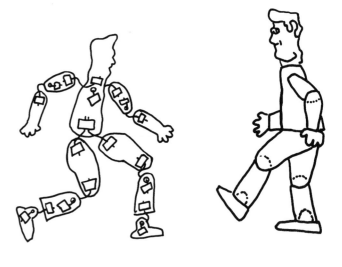

Sometimes you don't need hinges. In this long shot, the human character has no hinges. The diver was inserted into the scene by his air hose. The fish has one simple hinge at its tail.

This crab, which was made by a ten-year-old boy, has forty-four moving parts, but was hinged easily. He laid the thread down on the back of each grouping of segments, and put a piece of tape across each segment. This way, the crab could be animated to swim gracefully across the scene with very little work.

In some cases it is necessary to make loose hinges. Birds and chickens have a peculiar up-and-down movement when they walk, so their leg hinges need to have extra thread.

This gives you both the security of a hinged character and the flexibility of an unhinged one. As you move these characters, imagine that you are they, and think how you would move. Animators have to be like actors.

Automobiles, trucks, wheelbarrows, and anything else with wheels are easily animated by hinging the wheels with the hole-punching technique. Always tape these hinges tightly with very little play in the joints. You want the wheel to turn precisely on its axis.

The wheels themselves should be slightly uneven or have markings on the hubcap which will be noticeable when they turn. As you move the car forward a little, also turn the wheels a little. The larger the movement and the fewer frames taken for each movement, the faster the car appears to move.

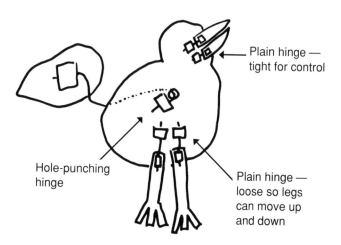

Plain hinge —
tight for control

Hole-punching
hinge

Plain hinge —
loose so legs
can move up
and down

Replacement Animation

In *replacement animation*, the characters are not hinged. Instead, multiple copies of them are made. In one scene, a car roars down a narrow street. This took eight separate cutout cars, each a little bigger than the one before it.

The scene below also uses replacement animation. The animator painted a series of heads turned in different directions. Since the heads were all the same size, a light outline showing the position of the head was drawn in pencil on the background.

The heads could be removed and replaced easily, using the outline as a guide. To make it look as if the stationary wheel was turning, the hands were moved along the wheel.

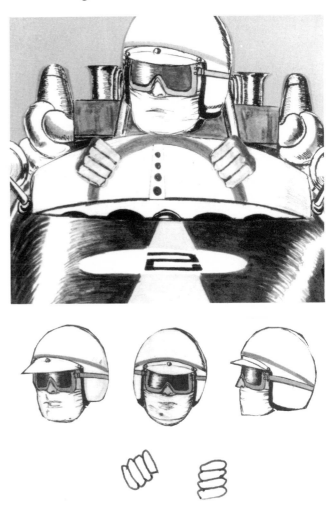

Easy Animation

There are other reasons for cutouts not to have hinges. If you show running people only from the waist up, you don't have to animate their legs. In the scene on below, the soldiers ran forward with a slight up-and-down motion. A curved dotted line below the frame of the picture helped the animator to estimate this movement.

This is not replacement animation, but carefully planned movement of stiff, unhinged characters.

If the soldiers all slid forward smoothly, it would not look like they were running. The elephant is standing still, but on the sound track we hear the elephants trumpeting and other sounds of war. The complete effect was created without too much work!

Medium Shots

Sometimes a film can be made without medium shots. You can get by with a title, followed by a long shot, a close-up, another long shot, and the end title. However, if the film is longer, and you want to vary the scenes somewhat, use a medium shot.

This scene of a television scientist explaining a complex machine is a typical medium shot. The figure is shown from the waist up. Some other samples can be found on pages 55 and 56.

Titles

Titles are important. The opening title is the first thing an audience sees.

They give information and can create a feeling of excitement. The beginning and end titles act like bookends, holding the story together.

Titles are the last scenes to be made, so if your story is not clear or it seems to lack a little snap, they give you another chance to solve these problems.

Sometimes a character from the film participates in the titles. The overcoated figure in *Super Sleuth* creates a mood of surprise and intrigue when he opens his coat to show the titles inside.

Lettering of titles should be simple, bold, and readable.

There are two techniques for lettering. In the *formal* way, you paint perfect letters directly on the page in exactly the right spot. This is a tricky process for most people. It's hard to calculate the exact position and size for each letter without having a lot of experience.

The *informal* technique is better for most beginners. Sketch the letters lightly with a pencil, cut them out of paper, and then paint them some solid color. You do not need to shape the letters evenly —just make them fat and very readable. If they are a little lumpy, that is part of the charm.

Sample film title

You can now lay these cutout letters on the page to see how they look. You may need to use a larger background paper, depending on the size of the letters. The words should be in the middle of the page, with a lot of space separating them from the edge. The background color should contrast with the letters.

It may take some time to cut out the letters, but in the long run you will have saved time and given yourself more options. You won't have spent time repainting titles until you got them right. You can rearrange the letters until they are satisfactory, and you can animate them.

A film title has three main parts: the name of the film, the name of the filmmaker, and the end title.

Parents and Families, a sponsored film made by a nine-year-old girl for the opening of the White House Conference on Children in 1970, starts with yellow letters on a red background.

This film follows the activities of a family throughout the day. At night, the little girl turns off the light, while saying "Good night." Then, the screen goes black.

This is another good way to indicate the end of the film.

Try to have short titles. However, when filming titles, estimate enough time for the audience to read them.

Audiences don't want to read a lot of words or to be told a story with words. They want to see the story in pictures!

A good rule is to shoot twenty-four frames of film for every major word in a title. If the scene turns out to be a little too long, you can always cut it shorter when you edit. A title scene that is too short to read must be refilmed.

Example: "THE END" in plain letters on a plain colored background.

Shoot three seconds of film, or three times twenty-four frames:

one second for "THE,"
one second for "END,"
one second for the background.

You will have a total of seventy-two frames.

If you move the letters onto the scene one at a time, shoot seventy-two frames after the movement stops. If the letters are still, but the background is complicated, the audience will need more time to read the titles. They will be distracted by the movement or the background, so film for a longer time.

In *I Wish*, a girl going to sleep sets the scene nicely for a series of dreams. The titles come out in a series of *"think" balloons*.

Sponges starts without the diver in the scene. The letters themselves were painted like sponges. The diver rises up from behind the cutout rock to gather up the letters. A ten-year-old boy made this informational film about sponges — where they are found, how they are gathered, and what they are used for. His last scene shows a hand using a sponge to suck up a watery "THE END." This is accompanied by a sucking noise on the sound track.

Sometimes it is useful to paint or paste the letters of the title onto clear animation cels.

Choose this technique when the lettering must be very formal or if it is to be laid on top of other artwork or photographs.

Use a field guide under the cels to help place the letters evenly. Line up the bottom of the letters on the lines of the field guide.

When using a field guide with a peg bar at the bottom, place it under the camera before filming to be sure the artwork is lined up. Then, tape the peg bar to the table.

Sand Animation

Sand animation is a technique that you can use to make a whole film. Usually, beach sand is laid on top of white plastic, and lighted from underneath. There should be no other lights on in the room.

Use a brush or your fingers to draw in the sand, pushing it away from the plastic. The sand films black, and the places with no sand on them film white.

This scene from a film about giraffes was lit from the top. The running giraffe kicks up the sand into the shape of the title.

The sound track for this sequence is of jungle drums. The giraffe was cut out from a magazine and hinged at the joints.

Filming Cutouts

The camera setup for filming cutouts is almost exactly the same as for flip books. The main difference is that cutout artwork is usually much larger. Film cameras take more on all four sides than the area you can see through the eyepiece, so you will need to zoom down to a smaller area. Video cameras will usually take the same area you see.

Focusing

If you are using a zoom lens, zoom in all the way to extreme close-up, focus, then zoom back out to your filming position. If you are using a 16mm Bolex, remember to open the lens all the way, to give yourself a lot of light when you focus.

The aperture ring on the lens controls the amount of light that comes in. The printed markings on it are called *f-stops*. When you turn the ring to a lower number such as 1.4, much more light enters than at a high number such as 16.

In filming cutouts, we frequently lay a sheet of nonglare glass on top of the paper characters to get them to lie flat and to get rid of shadows. Nonglare glass is a must for shiny surfaces such as animation cels. This inexpensive material can be bought at a glass supply house. Get a piece about two inches bigger on all four sides than your artwork.

Wrap a piece of black tape all around the sharp edges of the glass. Position the glass on top of the artwork. Attach the rear edge of the glass (above the top edge of the artwork) to the table with duct tape. You can then pick up and put down the front edge of the glass as if it were a flap. Make a little handle for the flap by doubling over a strip of duct tape and attaching it to the front side on the right.

Lighting

Super-8mm film cameras and video cameras have automatic *electric eyes* for determining the correct exposure. These work well for most scenes, but not for those that have a lot of black in them, such as a tiny spaceship in a black sky, or a dark city with snowflakes coming down.

The camera would misread all this black, and think that the scene was too dark. It would turn out overexposed, and would be gray, instead of black.

The remedy is to use a *gray card*. Lay the gray card on top of the artwork. Let the camera take its reading from the card. Then, "freeze" the EE (electric eye) reading so that when you remove the gray card the reading stays the same.

Bolex 16mm cameras require the use of a separate light meter to tell you what the correct lens opening should be. Remove the repro accessory, pushing the converter slide to the right. Point the light meter at the gray card on top of the artwork to measure the *reflected light*. Then, set the appropriate f-stop on the camera lens.

If you don't have a gray card, leave the repro accessory on the meter. Place the meter flat on the artwork, facing up toward the lights. Take a reading of the *incident light*.

Try to light the artwork very evenly. Have the lights far enough away and tilted properly so they don't cast a half circle of light on each side of the artwork.

Special Effects

Snow

You can create the effect of snow in many ways. Tiny cutout snowflakes were animated directly on top of the city buildings on the opposite page. Larger ones were animated on top of the scene below.

In this scene, cutout snowflakes were also used, but not on the artwork itself. The snowflakes were moved along a piece of clear glass placed about six inches above the artwork. This way, the angel's wings could still be moved.

You can also paint tiny snowflakes on a long, vertical sheet of clear acetate. Lay this on top of flat artwork, and move it downward. Place a strip of masking tape on the filming table along both sides of the acetate. Mark one strip like a ruler, to show how far the sheet must move every frame.

Lay a sheet of nonglare glass on top of the acetate to hold it flat and reduce its glare. Secure the glass to the table along one side with duct tape.

The camera must also have a black shield to keep its own reflection from appearing in the picture. You can make this shield from a piece of black cardboard in which you cut a hole for the camera lens to stick through.

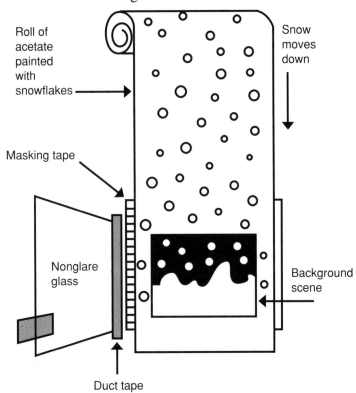

In the scene at left, snow appeared to accumulate on the tops of buildings because the animator painted four different city skylines, each one with more snow than the last.

Each skyline was filmed with the snow coming down on the acetate roll.

When a final print was made, the lab could *dissolve* between each section. In a dissolve, one scene gradually changes into the next scene.

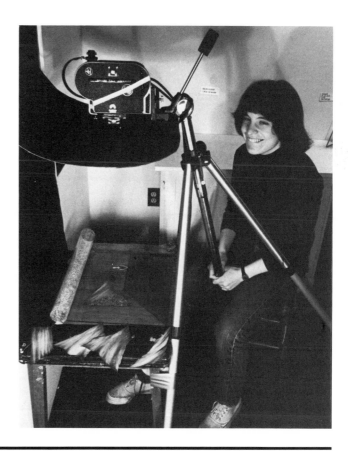

Rain

Rain can be produced in the same ways. You can cut out long, thin teardrop shapes, and lay them directly on the artwork, or draw streaks on a sheet of acetate. These streaks of rain are usually gray or black. Acrylic paint from an art supply store or *cel-vinyl* paint from an animation supply house will stick on acetate sheets.

If your scene starts as a sunny day, and turns rainy, be sure the bottom of the acetate has no rain on it. As you animate the sheet downward, the raindrops should gradually start to appear. Since you may have to lift up the nonglare glass occasionally, attach it to the table along the left edge with duct tape.

Roll up the acetate at top and bottom so it will stay out of your way when animating. The height of the roll depends on how long you want it to rain in the scene. You may be moving it downward about one-half inch every two frames. Most of the time, a height three times that of the artwork is enough.

Start with the acetate covering the artwork completely. Since this clear layer will make the scene a little darker, make sure it covers your whole drawing during the entire scene, or the edge of the acetate will show as it moves downward.

Cycles

You can also animate snow or rain using cycles, a series of numbered drawings which can be repeated over and over. This laborsaving device is used frequently in animation.

On the opposite page, the raindrops were a little lower on each acetate sheet, so that after filming the third drawing, the animator could begin the cycle again with the first drawing. Cycle drawings are registered, enabling them to be laid in exactly the same place each time.

The most accurate registration technique is to use twelve-field Acme punched animation cels. These sheets of clear acetate measure 10⅜ by 12½ inches and have registration holes punched into the bottom. You tape a white plastic Acme registration peg bar to the filming table just below the artwork and place the cels on the bar.

Another registration technique is to draw *cross hairs* (two small lines intersecting each other in the shape of an X) at the bottom corners of acetate sheets. You would also draw these same cross hairs on the filming table. Then you could match the crosses on the acetate with those on the table.

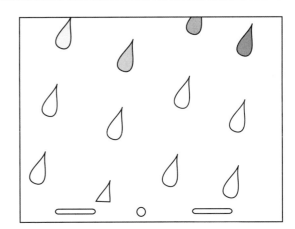

A three-sheet cycle is filmed in sequence: 1, 2, 3, 1, 2, 3, etc.

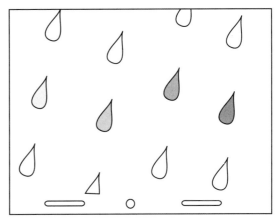

A cutout car drives through a cycle of rain. For this, different sheets of acetate were laid on top of the background, one at a time.

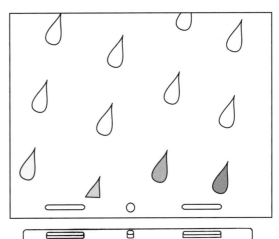

These sheets were registered (positioned) by fitting them onto the peg bar at the bottom.

Fire and Smoke

Scenes with constantly moving elements such as rain, snow, fire, smoke, and water are fun to watch, but require a lot of work. If you also have characters moving in these scenes, it's easier to have two animators. One can control the environment while the other moves the characters.

This scene from the film *Fat Feet* starts with a man going to sleep in an armchair. He drops his lighted cigarette, which makes the rug catch on fire.

Smoke and flames must be kept moving every two frames. Replacement technique was used for this. A small flame, a medium-size flame, and a large flame started the scene. After that, three large flames of different shapes were alternated for a while.

Animating smoke is a little different, as it not only changes shape but also moves upward and to one side. Some of the drawings of smoke could be reused, but many more different sizes needed to be made than in the case of the flames.

Splashes and Explosions

Here, a dragon dives into the water. A slit was cut along the line of a wave so the dragon could be inserted in it. Since you may have to film such scenes more than once, try to make the slit along a natural line to camouflage it.

At the point of impact, a series of cutout splashes were made. This same technique can be used for explosions. Sometimes, just three cutouts of splashes or an explosion are needed. You would film a sequence of small, medium, large, medium, and small splashes for two frames each.

Underwater Scenes

Suspend a container of water between the camera lens and the artwork. Dip your finger into the water to make it move. You can use glass-bottomed dishes if the brand name is not engraved on the bottom.

We use a picture frame with glass, and build up the edges with Plasticine. Prop this up in a secure position, and pour in water. Seal the edges carefully with Plasticine first, so water won't spill onto the artwork.

Since glass and water are reflective, a picture of the camera and animator may be included in the scene. To eliminate this, place a black shield between the camera lens and the glass container. We use a piece of cardboard with a hole for the camera lens.

Frame underwater scenes a little closer to the center of the picture than usual because moving water distorts the sides of the picture, making them look sucked in. If you find a good, clear piece of distorted glass, you can move this *ripple glass* between the lens and the artwork instead of using water.

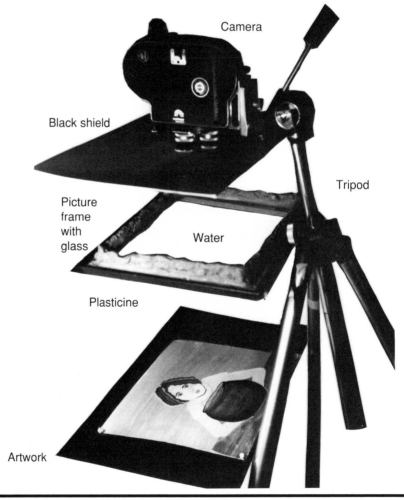

Camera

Black shield

Picture
frame
with
glass

Water

Tripod

Plasticine

Artwork

Zooms, Pans, and Tilts

Zooms

When you *zoom in*, the camera first takes in all of a scene, then moves gradually closer, until it takes in only a small portion.

When you *zoom out*, the camera first takes in only a small portion of the scene, then gradually takes in a larger area.

If you are using a zoom lens, plan your zooms to go straight into the *center* of your artwork, not to the side.

Shoot at least two seconds of the scene at the beginning of the shot before you begin to zoom in or out. After the zoom ends, shoot an additional two seconds.

Pans

A *pan* is movement horizontally across a wide landscape. In live-action filming, the *camera* moves across the scene. In animation, the camera remains motionless on its stand. The *artwork* is moved.

Position a strip of tape marked like a ruler on your filming table, along the bottom of the artwork. Move the artwork evenly along this tape, one or two frames for each mark.

If you have animation in a scene that is to be panned, it's a little more complex. In addition to moving the background, you have to animate the figures.

Here, the boy and girl began on the right side of the scene. The background did not move. The camera held on the scene for two seconds, while the boy turned and walked off to the left with the girl. At this point, the background started moving to the right. The characters moved with it — the girl pedaling her bicycle, the boy walking, and the kite flying. In such a scene, your job is to *keep the characters always in the center of the page.*

The camera operator must keep checking the position of the characters through the lens. It is helpful to tape a strip of paper at the front edge of your filming table. Each time, before you move the background, bend that strip up *in front of* where you want the first character to be.

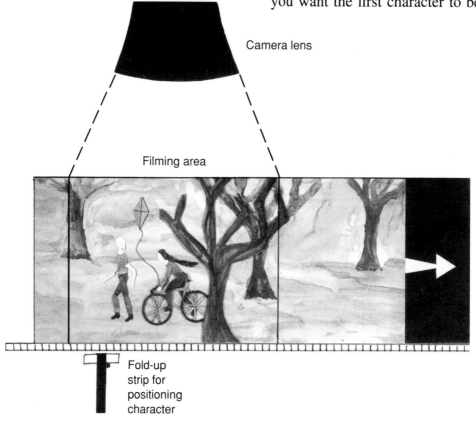

Camera lens

Filming area

Fold-up strip for positioning character

Then, animate the scene by moving the background and by moving the characters forward to the edge of the strip. Bend the strip back down out of the way and take the frames.

Tilts

A *tilt* is a vertical pan up or down a landscape. You can achieve the effect of a sunrise behind a house by painting a long, vertical background. Tape the cutout house and lawn to the filming table at the edges of the lawn. Filming starts with the dark part of the sky behind the house. Move the background slowly upward.

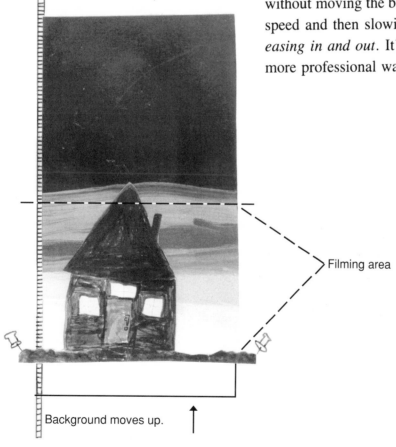

Filming area

Background moves up.

Easing In and Out

Start filming without moving the landscape for two seconds. Then move it just a tiny bit, one frame at a time, for about twelve frames. Then move it a full *increment* each frame, until you get close to the end of the scene. An increment is whatever length you have decided to move the background each time — a quarter inch, a half inch, or some other measurement. Mark these off on the tape on the side before beginning to film.

At this point, start slowing down again. When you get to the end of the scene, film for two seconds without moving the background. This getting up to speed and then slowing down at the end is called *easing in and out*. It's considered a smoother and more professional way to pan, tilt, and zoom.

5 Special Techniques for Flat Animation

Photographs

Animation is the creation of a new world. You can do this by making drawings or sculptural objects. You can also manipulate existing things, such as photographs or pictures from magazines. At left, the city buildings seen through the window started as a photograph. Then, the animator made photocopies of it and painted on it with watercolor. Some details were outlined with a black pen. The man, the smoke, and the window are watercolor paintings.

The cutout film *Racing Practice* has a scene with a side-view mirror. Reflected in it is a driver speeding to overtake the hero.

The driver below was made out of a photo from a magazine. To make it look like the car was moving, the animator slid the photo around behind a hole cut in a painting of a side-view mirror. This is easy but effective animation.

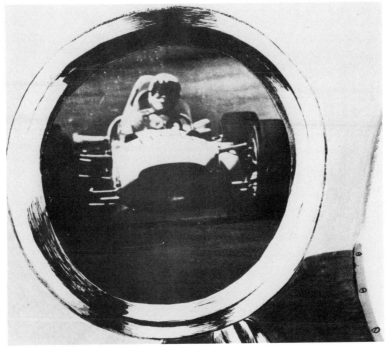

The Wedding recorded a real event in black-and-white still photographs.

Later, an animator reconstructed the wedding. A reception line was formed with cutouts of people taped to a colored background.

Here, in the picture below, an older woman passes behind the hosts of the party and says to the bride, "Such a lovely wedding!"

The only animation in this scene was the moving of the old woman and the placement of a slightly open cutout mouth on top of her own mouth.

The animator placed the mouth on the face and then removed it every two frames to synchronize with the words. This was a close-up scene, so the woman's feet did not have to move.

The sentence is divided into syllables.

"Such........a........love......ly......wed......ding!"

OO — O — OO - O — OO — O

Each oval represents two frames of a partly opened mouth. Each dash represents two frames of a closed mouth. It takes thirty-four frames for the woman to say this sentence.

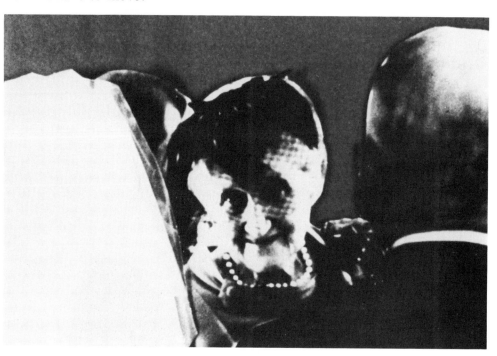

In this scene, another woman drinks punch. It's a little stronger than she expected.

The only animation needed was the placement of two round, surprised eyes on top of her existing eyes.

The new eyes rotate completely around as the woman exclaims, "Oh, my!"

Xerography

Xerography involves photocopying magazines or photographs.

You can make progressively larger or smaller copies to create the effect of something approaching the camera or going away from it.

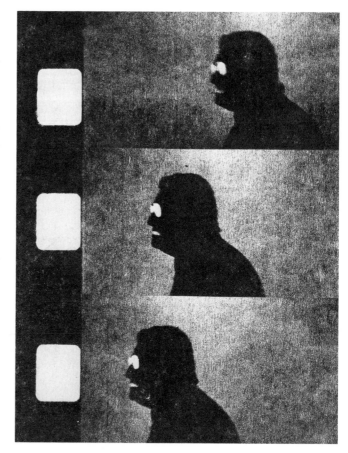

Frames from super-8mm or 16mm movie film can be copied to paper on microfiche machines. The one we use can copy the picture as a positive or a negative, larger or smaller, and darker or lighter.

When you copy an image from film, it is best to print the perforations along the edges of the frame as well, so you can use them to help you register the image.

Xerography is a lot of fun. When you copy 16mm or super-8mm film onto paper, it's like a treasure hunt. You never know how the printed image is going to turn out. It always looks different from the original film because it gets more contrast. Everything becomes either black or white. There are no grays. You get some interesting and dramatic images.

We put a super-8mm film of a girl looking into a mirror in a microfiche machine and printed one of the frames onto paper. Then we cut the contrasty face out of the paper and gave it new shoulders and a hat. It suggested a man walking in a city at night, so we looked for a background scene to fit the character.

Rotoscoping

Rotoscoping is the process of filming a live-action event, projecting it one frame at a time, and tracing the movement. These drawings have very realistic movement.

Rotoscoped characters can be changed and put into different backgrounds. For example, a person walking down the street can be given horns and a tail.

Using a close-up film scene of a person making faces at the camera, you can change the face to look like a clown.

A man dances. If you trace just the outline of his body and move the paper over, you can trace another copy of him dancing next to himself. This way, you've created two men dancing in unison.

Equipment Needed

In super 8mm the simplest setup uses a super-8mm viewer. For our first project of this kind we filmed polar bears at the zoo in super-8mm film.

After the film was developed, we loaded it into the super-8mm viewer and stopped on the first frame of the movement. Then we cut twenty-six pieces of clear acetate to the size that would fit into the screen of the viewer, and numbered them in the corner.

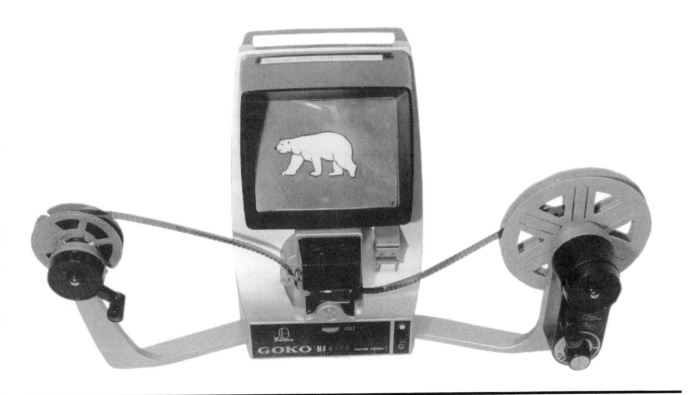

After tracing the image of the bear onto the acetate using a thin-tipped marker, we moved the film forward to the next frame, leaving the first drawing on the viewer. We could see that the bear did not move very much between the first frame and the second frame, so we decided to draw every other frame. Then, we turned the drawings over and painted the bears white on the underside.

We found background scenes of ice and snow in a magazine. The next step was to make a little frame around the background with black tape, so that every time I put down another drawing of the bear, it would be in the right position.

We filmed the first bear for twenty-four frames, or one second, standing still. Each of the other drawings was filmed for three frames. The last one was filmed for twenty-four frames.

The bear moved differently than he did in real life because we had control of his movements. He could move faster or slower. We used cel-vinyl paint from an animation supply company. However, you could also use acrylic paint.

Other Ways to Rotoscope

Some super-8mm or 16mm projectors can project one frame at a time. Load the film into the projector and project the frames onto paper or clear acetate taped to a wall. Using this technique, you can work at a larger size than with a viewer, but the shadow of your hand may be in the way of the projected image.

You can eliminate this shadow with *rear projection*. Project the image onto a piece of *ground glass* or frosted acetate held in a frame. Place your paper or clear acetate on the other side of the frame to trace the image.

You can also set the projector on the floor, with a mirror braced at a 45-degree angle in front of it. Cut a hole in an old table and set a piece of ground glass into it. The projector beams the image to the mirror and up through the ground glass. Put your paper or acetate over the glass to trace the image.

In a pinch, you can rotoscope from a video monitor if your VCR can stop a frame and advance one frame at a time.

Rear Projection

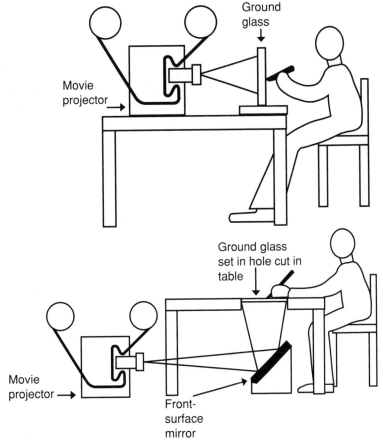

Ground glass

Movie projector

Ground glass set in hole cut in table

Movie projector

Front-surface mirror

Editing Polaroid super-8mm instant movie film
for rotoscoping

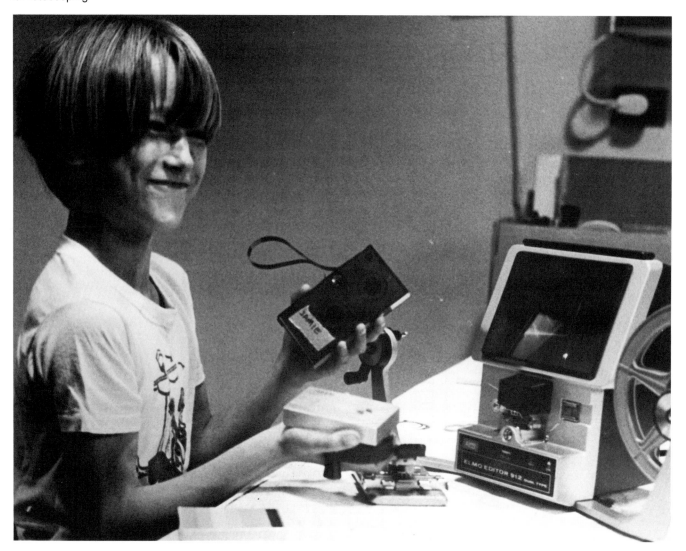

A ten-year-old girl drew this rotoscoped horse with a black Staedtler Lumocolor S313 permanent marker. You can erase lines made with these markers by using rubbing alcohol on a cotton swab.

The most elegant way to rotoscope in super 8mm is to own the Polaroid Slow Motion Stop Action Player. You can shoot live-action scenes using the Polaroid Instant Movie Camera or a regular super-8mm camera, and then splice the film into the Polaroid cassette. The viewer looks like a small television screen. You can also shoot live action on a regular super-8mm camera and then splice the film into the Polaroid cassette.

We cut the screen out with a pair of scissors and set our own frame in front of it. Our frame has clear, hard plastic with a sheet of frosted acetate on it for a screen. A registration peg at the bottom holds twelve-field animation cels. These machines are not made anymore, so you can only use this technique if you own one already.

A J.K. optical printer is an excellent rotoscoping machine. It has a projector on one end that can project 16mm or super-8mm film onto a mirror. If you are lucky enough to own this unit, put it on the floor under a table like the diagram on page 77.

An advantage of this printer is that it has a remote-control pedal, so that you can sit at the table and press the pedal to move the frame forward or backward.

Polaroid Slow Motion Stop Action Player

Frame with plastic screen

6   Stories and Storyboards

Stories have beginnings, middles, and ends. If you know what these are in advance, it will help your work. Most people can start a story with a few characters and make something interesting happen to the characters, but it's harder to make a satisfactory ending — to bring the story to a conclusion in an interesting way.

A storyboard is helpful for animators. A rough sketch of the scenes in a film in the order they will appear, it's a bit like a comic book. Under the pictures appear the words and descriptions of the action and the sounds. Storyboards can help you to make a good story and to see how your shots will look next to each other.

It's possible to start making an animated film without having a story in mind first. That way you figure it out as you go along. This technique is fine for an artist working alone. If you are working with other people or have a limited amount of time and money to spend, you will want to plan carefully and make a storyboard first.

A storyboard is like a road map. You look at it and check off the scenes you have already made. Some scenes can be assigned to other people to make. You can figure out the cost of the film if you know what all the scenes will look like and how long they will be.

In the Middle is an original story based on personal experiences.

There is not much animation in the film. Just one or two things move in each scene.

This humorous and poignant story is narrated in the slightly quavery voice of the young girl who wrote, painted, and animated the story.

Once, there was a girl who always liked to look around.

She would look everywhere.

She had to look down at people and up at people.

She was too old not to do any chores.

She was too old to go to the little school, too young to go to the big school.

Vroom, Vroom, Vroom! She was too young to drive a car.

Waah! Waah! She was too old to cry and too young to go to a psychiatrist!

One day another girl came along.

The girl said, "Hi!"

And they were just the right age to be friends. The End.

Robert's Levi's Commercial

This commercial for Levi's was made by a junior-high student for Robert's Children's Clothing store. A storyboard was essential because the film had to be exactly thirty seconds long for television. Time and money were limited, and the client had to approve the story.

Scene 1: Long shot
Action: Camera zooms in to porthole of spaceship.
Sound: Humming noise made by child.

Scene 2: Medium shot
Action: Alien hands point downward to earth.
Sound: Chattering chipmunks.

Scene 3: Long shot
Action: Spaceship lands. Crowd pours into Robert's store.
Sound: Roar of spaceship, galloping of aliens.

Scene 4: Medium shot
Action: Saleswoman screams as aliens rush to her rack of Levi's trousers.
Sound: Scream, galloping.

Scene 5: Long shot
Action: Smiling aliens leave store.
Sound: Voice-over: "Some kids come a big distance..."

Scene 6: Close-up
Action: Satisfied alien pats his Levi label.
Sound: "...to get Levi's at Robert's!"

Scene 7: Long shot
Action: Spaceship takes off in cloud of smoke.
Sound: Roar of spaceship. Saleswoman screaming, "Come back soon!"

Scene 8: Long shot
Action: Spaceship in space.
Sound: Hum getting softer.

A special problem when shooting film for showing on television is the TV cutoff. This means that television screens show a smaller area than film projectors do. It's necessary to plan the artwork so there is extra space around the four sides.

You can lay special field guides, which show TV cutoff areas, over your artwork to show you how much will be cut off when the image is broadcast.

Film format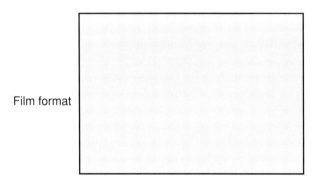

TV format

TV cutoff area

Super Sleuth, shown below, is a crime story. These are fun to make, as everybody is already familiar with the basic framework, or plot. It's the filmmaker's job to make interesting variations on this.

Super Sleuth (SS) opens coat to show titles.
Sound: Music

SS hides behind newspaper.

SS enters men's room to get secret message from roll of toilet paper.
Sound (from toilet): "Good morning!"

Sound continues:
"Hal Mathot is planning another caper. Your job is to stop the Mathot Gang. This message will self-destruct...FLUSH!"

One of the gang forges a check to collect $400,000 at bank. He asks teller to put money in brown paper bag, and leaves for airport. SS follows him on bus.

Crook disappears in the crowd. SS finds out from ticket agent that gangster is on flight 216, leaving in five minutes.

Plane takes off with SS screaming and running after it. Gangster grins and waves from window of plane.

A discouraged SS returns to bank, where apologetic bank teller tells him there was a mistake. The crook took the wrong bag — his lunch.

Below is part of the actual storyboard for *The Life of John Doe,* a science-fiction comedy made as a group project by junior-high students. The film contains both live action with special effects and animation.

The live-action scenes required the construction of a city park, an underground cavern, a mad scientist's laboratory, and the huge head of a dragon capable of swallowing a live boy. Many different jobs needed to be done, and the storyboard was constantly used for reference.

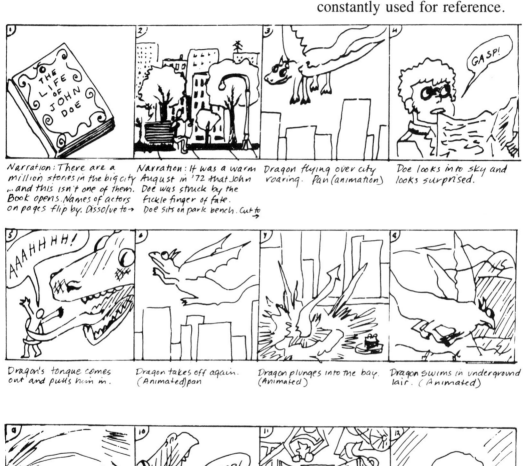

Narration: There are a million stories in the big city ...and this isn't one of them. Book opens. Names of actors on pages flip by. Dissolve to→

Narration: It was a warm August in '72 that John Doe was struck by the fickle finger of fate. Doe sits on park bench. Cut to→

Dragon flying over city roaring. Pan (animation)

Doe looks into sky and looks surprised.

Dragon's tongue comes out and pulls him in.

Dragon takes off again. (Animated) pan

Dragon plunges into the bay. (Animated)

Dragon swims in underground lair. (Animated)

He emerges into underground lair. Mouth opens. (Animated)

Doe and his captor, Egore, step out. Doe... "That was indeed a strange experience." Live action, with moving water matted in.

They enter scientific chamber where professor is working. Doe ... "Amazing!"

Prof... "Isn't it though! Let me introduce myself. Professor Menglet Fun Fuz Shmiot. Mad genius and war criminal. I have brought you here to show you my plans for conquering the world!"

Three-dimensional Animation

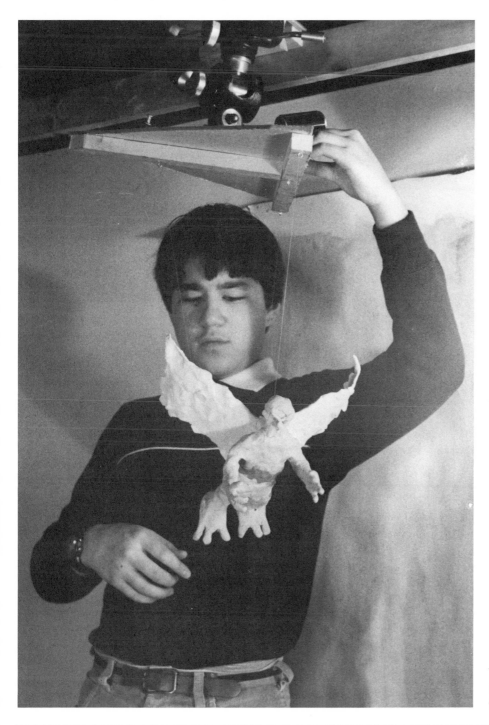

The animation of thick objects such as puppets and clay is called *three-dimensional animation*.

7 Clay Animation

The Set

The filming setup for clay animation is different from that for flat animation. The camera points horizontally at a set on a table. If the camera is more than three feet away from the set, you don't need close-up diopters for your lens.

The ground area for an average-size set can be a rectangular sheet of Masonite or plywood about thirty by twenty-four inches. Clamp the front corners of this set to the table using *C clamps* or duct tape.

Make your characters between four and ten inches tall. They should not be top-heavy. Think of them as people with big feet and small heads. Plasticine, which you will use to make the characters, is heavy, so they will have a tendency to fall over if they have big heads.

We use Harbutt's colored Plasticine. It's inexpensive and comes in one-pound boxes in sixteen different colors. Sometimes, we insert an *armature,* or framework, of aluminum wire inside the bodies, although this is not always necessary.

You can cover the ground of the set with a thin layer of Plasticine, or build up hilly areas around which the character can walk. Construct buildings and caves roughly from cardboard, tape them together, and then cover them with a layer of Plasticine.

The sky is usually painted on a separate piece of heavy white paper and hung on the wall in back of the set. You will need to leave at least twelve inches of space between this background paper and the back of the set, so paint the paper wider than the width of the set. The camera will be able to see more of it since it is farther away.

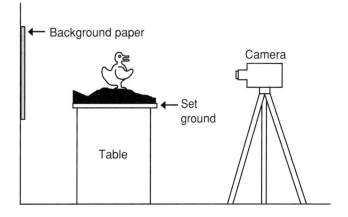

Lighting

You need from three to five lights for this type of animation. One just lights the sky separately, so no shadows will fall on it from the characters, trees, or buildings. Clamp a 250-watt light on something above the set, so it can point down at the sky.

We use a lighting boom (see p. 22) for this.

You also need a strong overall light of 500 watts or more. Position this *key light* near the camera, pointing at the set.

Then you need at least one other light, a *fill light* of 250 watts, for the left side. It's helpful to have one of these for the right side, too. Sometimes, an extra small light is needed to illuminate some special portion of the set, such as inside a building.

The camera does not see the front corners of the set because of *sight lines* (the area within range of the camera, as shown in the diagram). At these corners C clamps hold the set to the table.

Lighting and perspective diagram
(overhead view)

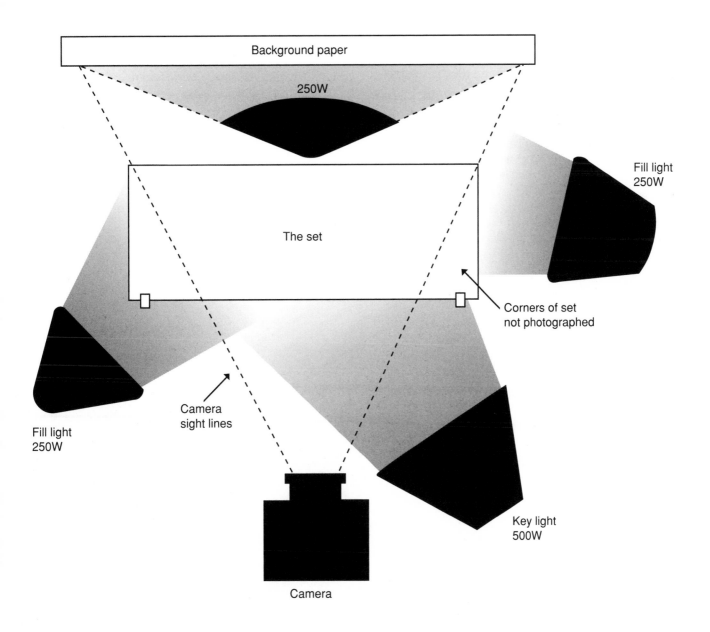

Background paper

250W

Fill light
250W

The set

Corners of set
not photographed

Camera
sight lines

Fill light
250W

Key light
500W

Camera

Depth of Field

Lighting is important because the atmosphere of the scene relies on it. What will be in or out of focus depends partially on the amount of light available. This is called *depth of field.*

When you were filming flat things, it was easy to focus because everything was on the same level, or plane. A set for clay animation is thick. Some things are in the front, and some in the back. If you focus the camera on something in the front, the items in the back will be in *soft focus,* or blurred.

For example, if you set your lens to focus on something twenty inches away, everything between eighteen and twenty-two inches may be in focus. That four-inch area is your depth of field. Things closer or farther away may be out of focus, or outside your depth of field.

If you don't have much light, your depth of field gets shorter. If you have a lot of light, the area in sharp focus may be deeper.

Film and Video Stock

We prefer Kodachrome 40 in super 8mm because the quality of the copies is better, but since this film has an *ASA* (light sensitivity) of only 40, you will need stronger lights. For this reason we shoot clay sets with Ektachrome 160 so our clay characters don't melt!

In 16mm we use Ektachrome 7240 film, or any color film with an ASA of 125 or more. Even though videotape can record an image in dim light, you can increase the quality of the image and the depth of field with proper lighting.

Now that you know roughly what sizes to make the characters and sets, you can concentrate on making them. We usually slice the one-pound blocks of Plasticine into smaller segments and put these pieces under one of the filming lights to soften them. Place the Plasticine at least eighteen inches from the lights. Leave it there until it is easy to

manipulate. Plasticine becomes more workable as you handle it.

Try to make a simple character with very little texture. Striped pants and polka-dotted shirts will get damaged when you press the character to move him to another position. The character gets a lot of his personality from the way he moves, rather than from how complex he looks.

If you want the character to walk around a lot, it might be a good idea to embed an armature of aluminum wire in him. This will allow for a lot of handling while helping to keep the character tall enough.

This man, who walked around and tipped his hat, had no wire until it was time for him to lift the heavy clay hat off his head. At that time we inserted a short section of wire through the hat and the arm, all the way into the body and across the shoulders.

Acting

In clay animation it is most important for you to project yourself into the body of the character. You must be an actor. As you move the character, you must become him. His spinal column must be yours. You must enter his body, feel his feelings, and express his emotions. You must feel his feet firmly pressed to the ground for balance.

Three-dimensional animation is quite theatrical in quality. The character must have a lively personality.

Thinking of your character as an actor, imagine how he enters the scene. What are his eyes looking at? Eyes are important. Characters get a lot of personality from their eyes.

Does the character stand out from the background? Is he well lighted? Does he have his back to the camera? If this is necessary for part of the scene, be sure the audience has a chance to see his face at some point.

As you are animating the character, keep looking through the camera to see how he looks.

Shots

As in all films, three-dimensional animation uses long shots, medium shots, and close-ups. You could just build one set and move the camera in closer or zoom in to create these effects, or you could actually build different sets for the long and medium shots and the close-up scenes.

This set for a television commercial for Robert's Children's Clothing store uses a medium shot for the main character, a child who likes to cook. In the film he makes a mess mixing the ingredients.

As the cookies are burning in the oven, he exclaims, "I think maybe I want to be a cook when I grow up!" Smelling the smoke, his mother enters the room. She screams, "Look at your clothes!" The boy says, "Oh, Mom, we can always go to Robert's and get me new ones!"

8 Puppetry Techniques

Cloth Characters

Puppets can be made of almost anything, including wood, foam rubber, wire, and cloth. In the past, the bodies of many puppets were made of wood, and their clothing, cloth. These days, some hand puppets are made of cloth stuffed with foam rubber. Puppets used for animation must also have a skeleton of flexible wire.

A technique that requires the sewing of cloth was used by the Yellow Ball Workshop for the film *The Great Green Planet*. The students drew astronauts on an old white sheet. We asked them to make the drawings much fatter than usual, in order to leave room for the stuffing. Then, they doubled over the cloth and sewed up the sides of each character, leaving an opening at the top of the head. They turned the characters inside out, and stuffed them with a wire armature and tiny pieces of cut foam rubber. The helmets were made of silver contact paper.

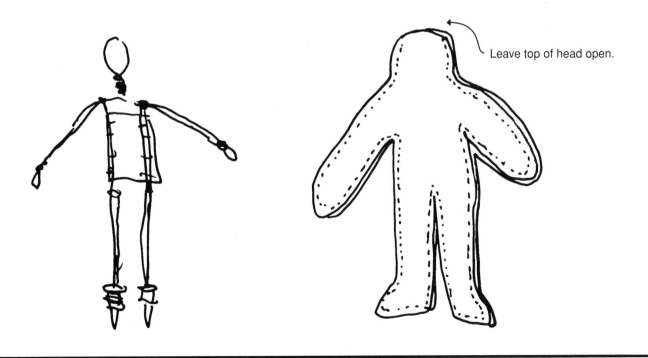

Leave top of head open.

Relief

A *relief* is a flat scene in which some parts stick up. You point the camera down at the artwork on a low table.

These large close-up heads are about ten inches high. The animators made replacement mouths from black, red, and white velvet contact paper. They constructed the hands from heavy paper with wire taped on back, and the arms from cloth wrapped around heavy cardboard, also with wire taped on back. They stuffed the cloth faces with lumps of movable cut foam rubber. The relief scene was filmed flat, in the same way as for cutouts.

Stand-up Cutouts

A cutout paper doll that is hinged in the back with wire instead of thread makes a very strange and magical type of puppet.

Wrap thin wire around pushpins in the area of the feet, and run it up the body. Then, paint a back view, and paste it to the back of the character to hide the wire.

These cutout characters are capable of a lot of movement. When they turn to the side, they get thin.

The female puppets in this photo have wire throughout their skirts, which bend around their legs as they walk.

Cut Foam Characters

In the summer of 1987, we took six American children to Yerevan, Armenia, U.S.S.R. to collaborate on puppet animation with six Armenian children. The project was sponsored by various groups, including International Arts for Peace.

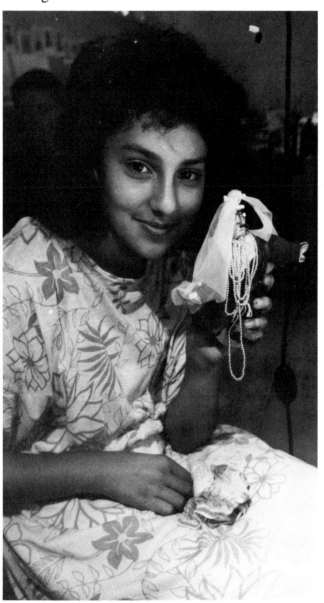

The film, entitled *The Golden Ball,* was based on the Armenian folktale about an unhappy rich couple who were always fighting and a poor family with a happy secret. Ahead of time we researched the costumes, art, and architecture found in Armenia in earlier days.

Then, we figured out an inexpensive way for a group of beginners to make lightweight characters in a short time. The techniques had to be both fun to do and easily explained through a translator.

Almost everything was stapled or taped together.

Pushpins were stuck through the bottom of the feet and into a ground made of Styrofoam.

Since these characters require almost no sewing, they can be made in about four hours.

Large white map tacks were used for the characters' eyes. The students painted pupils for the eyes on the tacks with acrylic paint. You may find these tacks in some stationery stores and arts-and-crafts shops.

Nose and mouth were painted directly onto the face.

The women wore beaded jewelry from an arts-and-crafts shop.

The first step in creating cut foam characters is to make a pencil sketch of how you expect them to look. Then, gather the supplies and tools.

Tools

Scissors, Ace Clipper stapler, matte knife, sewing needle

Supplies

Aluminum wire, ¹⁄₁₆″ thick........................for skeleton (armature)
Piece of foam rubber, ¼″ thick ....for body thickening
Double-stick tape ....for body and clothes
Cloth..for costume
Woman's stocking ....for head
Styrofoam slab, 1″ thick..for head
Acrylic paints ....for face
White map tacks for eyeballs......................................for face
DMC Mouline Special embroidery thread #25 ....for hair
Dark thread ....for hair
Long-shank aluminum pushpins, ¾″ ....for feet
Small sheet of foam core, ⅛″ ....for feet
Black masking tape..for feet

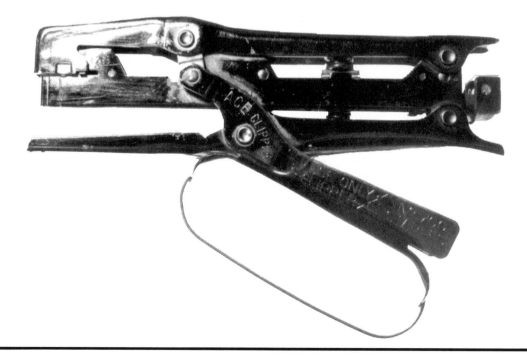

Legs

Wrap one end of the armature wire several times around the handle of the pushpin to create one foot. Estimate length of legs and body, and how much more wire you will need to wrap around the other foot. Cut this length, and wrap the wire around the other foot.

Body

Cut a rectangular piece of foam core for the torso of the body. Staple the legs to it using the Ace Clipper stapler. Cut a piece of wire long enough for both arms, including a loop for each hand. Staple this to the body. Staple a neck wire to the body.

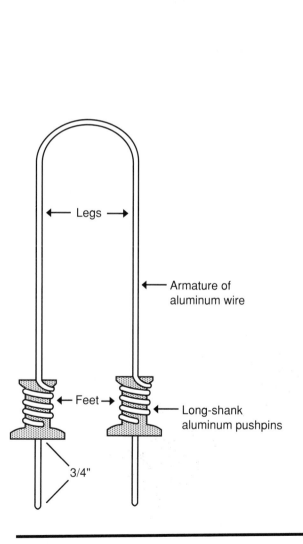

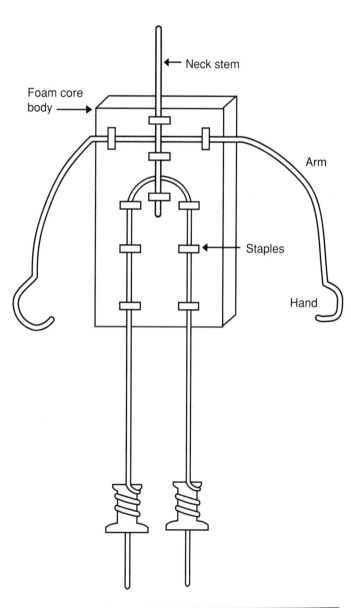

Heads

Cut a head shape out of a slab of Styrofoam. Stretch an old nylon stocking over it, tying it in the back with sewing thread. Stick the head onto the wire neck of the body.

Then, paint the face with acrylic paint, and let it dry. You may need to use more than one coat of paint. When the face is dry, sew the hair onto the head at the part, from the top of the head down the back.

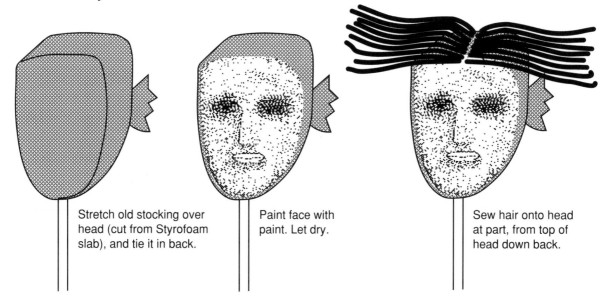

Stretch old stocking over head (cut from Styrofoam slab), and tie it in back.

Paint face with paint. Let dry.

Sew hair onto head at part, from top of head down back.

Feet

Cut a piece of foam core in the shape of a foot. Press a pushpin through this shape and through some black tape on the bottom of the foot. Fold this tape up and over the foot and the pushpin. The tape can also wrap around the bottom of the foam leg.

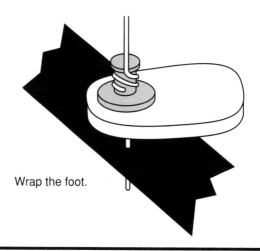

Wrap the foot.

Thickening the Body

Cut pieces of thin foam long enough to cover the front and back of the torso. Using double-stick tape, fasten them to the body.

Cut more pieces of foam, making them long enough to fold over each arm and leg, trimming the inside of the arms and legs on a diagonal. Lay a piece of double-stick tape along the edges of the foam and press the pieces together to seal them around the wire.

Push a second layer of black tape through the push-pin under the foot and wrap the tape over the foot to cover the bottom of the leg.

Hands

Cut out a hand from the foam core in the shape of a mitten. Stick the wire that extends from the wrist up through the hand and then back down through it, making a loop.

Dress the Character

Cut out squares of cloth. Fasten them together as rolls, using double-stick tape on the inside. Insert the arms and legs of the puppet into these tubes and fasten the tubes directly to the body with tape. Make the tunic a long rectangle with a hole in the middle for the head to go through. Fasten the sides together with double-stick tape.

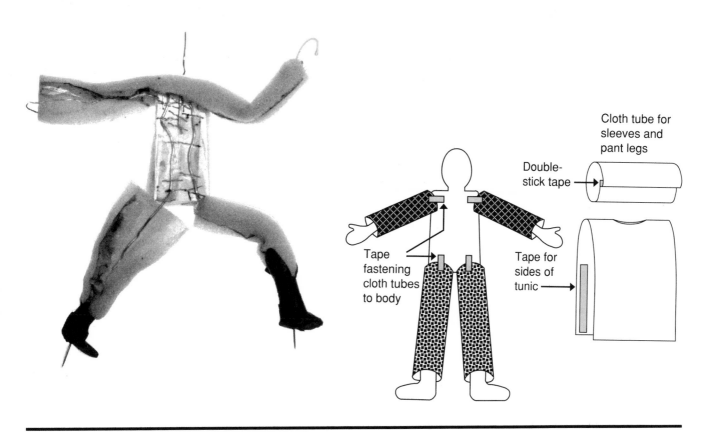

Cloth tube for sleeves and pant legs

Double-stick tape

Tape fastening cloth tubes to body

Tape for sides of tunic

Casting Liquid Foam Characters

The technique for making characters out of liquid foam rubber is more complex than that for cut foam. The advantage is that you can get a rather professional-looking character, which you have sculpted exactly the way you want it, and you can cast copies of it.

However, casting characters in liquid foam takes practice and experience. Supplies are more expensive, plaster can be messy, a stove is needed, and the process is more time-consuming.

Begin by making the character out of Plasticine. Then, make a two-part plaster mold of the Plasticine character. When the plaster is dry, shape an armature of aluminum wire, using pushpins for the feet. This armature must be able to fit into one of the halves of the plaster mold without touching the sides of it.

Prepare a mixture of liquid foam and lay it in the two halves of the mold. Lay the armature on one half, and tie the halves of the mold together with wire. Then cook this in an oven. Allow it to cool and then remove the mold. Inside, you will find a character made of foam rubber with an armature within it. (Supplies are listed on page 115.)

Plaster Mold

Make your first character a simple, two-legged one, so that you can make a two-part plaster mold.

Be sure not to have any *undercuts*, or places where the plaster curls around the character. If there is an undercut at the *parting line* you won't be able to get the character out. The parting line is the place where the two parts of the plaster mold separate. This line runs along the sides of the character at its widest point.

Correct

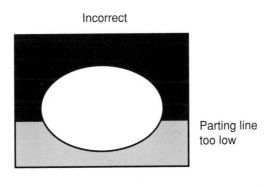

Top of
plaster mold

Parting line

Bottom of
plaster mold

Egg
character

Incorrect

Parting line
too low

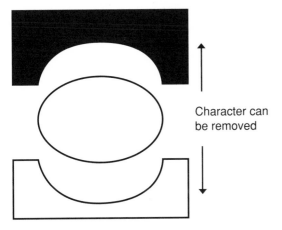

Character can
be removed

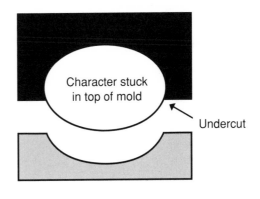

Character stuck
in top of mold

Undercut

After making your character out of Plasticine, spray it with three coats of Crystal Clear. Then lay it on a Masonite board on which you have placed lumps of water-soluble clay to raise the character off the surface of the board. Let the Crystal Clear dry.

Build up water-soluble clay around the character so that it looks as if it were half submerged in water. This "water line" will be the parting line.

The character usually sticks out the most at the parting line. BE SURE YOU DON'T MAKE ANY UNDERCUTS OR INDENTATIONS!

Make some triangular holes in the clay on either side of the body (see diagram below). You will use these later as alignment keys.

After you build up the sides, wrap a rubber mat around them, and secure it with duct tape.

Body of character

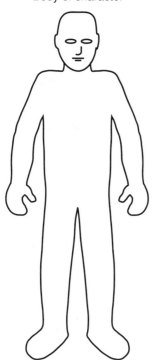

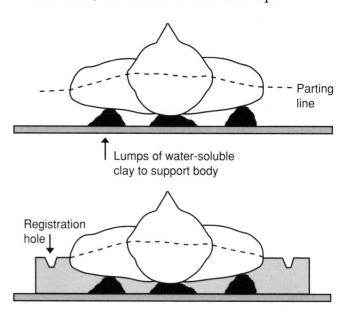

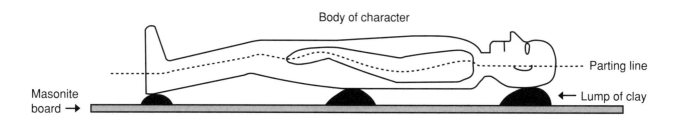

Coat the exposed insides of the rubber mat, the top of the character, and the top of the water-soluble clay with a thin layer of petroleum jelly. You can apply this to the character with a soft brush.

Mix up some plaster. Use Ultra Cal 30, not household plaster. You can purchase this type of gypsum cement at construction companies. It dries very strong and smooth in texture. Mix it in a bowl of water with your hands.

After mixing the plaster, pour it into the mold. The rubber mat around the sides will contain it.

Shake the whole mold to be sure there are no air bubbles.

Getting ready to pour Ultra Cal 30 into first half of plaster mold

Rubber mat taped around mold

Embedded character coated with petroleum jelly

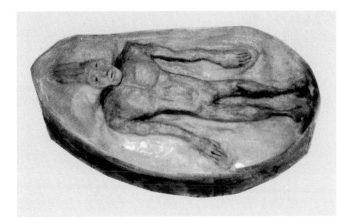

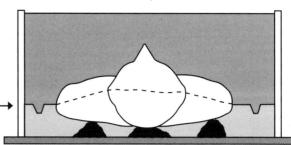

First half of plaster mold

When the plaster has hardened, but not completely cooled off, remove the rubber mat. Turn the mold over to start work on the back side, and remove the water-soluble clay.

Rubber mat →

When the plaster is completely hard and cool, clean up the exposed surface of the character and the mold (making minor repairs to the character and removing bits of water-soluble clay from the mold). Coat the character and the exposed plaster mold with a new layer of petroleum jelly.

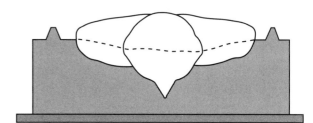

Second half of plaster mold

Tape the rubber mat around them. Coat the exposed inside of the rubber mat with petroleum jelly. Mix up a second batch of plaster, and pour it in. Shake it to get rid of air bubbles.

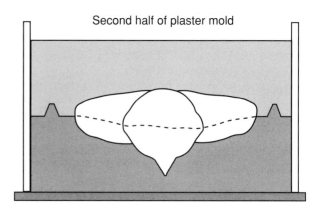

When the plaster is hard, take the rubber mat off, and separate the two sections of the mold. Take out the Plasticine character.

Clean the two sections of the plaster mold with a stiff brush. Be sure to remove all traces of Plasticine and petroleum jelly. Make an armature of aluminum wire that will fit inside the mold. Be sure to wrap the armature around the pushpins at the feet.

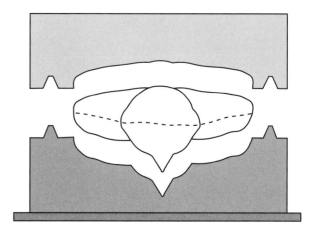

Wrap this armature around the shoulders and hips twice each. You may have to use two strands for the legs if the wire isn't thick enough.

If your character has a fat stomach, fit a thin piece of foam rubber inside the armature in the area of the stomach to create a bulge when you put it into the plaster mold.

In Hollywood, armatures have metal ball-and-socket construction. This is very expensive, and is not necessary for amateur films. Using aluminum wire and pushpins, you can make a sturdy character easily and inexpensively.

Lay the armature in the bottom section of the mold. It will be placed there after the foam has been put in. Does it fit perfectly? The metal should not scrape against the sides of the mold. There will be very little time to fool around with placing the armature after the foam has been inserted. Prepare the fit now!

You will need to make some scratches in the mold under the feet, to accommodate the points of the pushpins.

Coat both sections of the mold with *mold release*. When you do this, include all surfaces of the plaster where it will touch the other half or the foam.

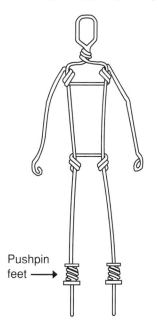

Armature of aluminum wire

Pushpin feet ⟶

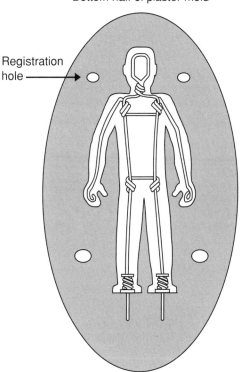

Bottom half of plaster mold

Registration hole ⟶

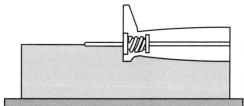

Cross section of pushpin positioned in thin groove scratched into lower half of mold.

Mix the liquid foam with an inexpensive hand-held electric mixer. The instructions come with the four bottles of ingredients. When the foam reaches the consistency of shaving cream, spoon it into both halves of the mold, being sure not to create any air bubbles. Lay the armature into the mixture in the mold of the character's back.

Carefully fit the halves of the mold together, fitting the alignment keys into the holes. Stand on top of the mold until the surface of the foam sets. You will know this has happened when the leftover mixture in the bowl has developed a skin.

Put the mold into a preheated oven for four hours at 200°F. Open the door and let the oven cool off before removing the mold.

The next day, remove the character from the mold and cut the thin skin from the edges with cuticle scissors. The character should be able to stand up when you press the pushpins of his feet into heavy cardboard or dense foam.

When you press the character's flesh in with your finger, it should pop back out. If it doesn't, it has no *memory*. This means that the foam has been improperly *cured*, or set, and you have to try again. Many factors can influence the quality of the foam: the temperature of the room; the speed, size, and type of electric mixer; the length of mixing time; the amount of formula used; and the length of cooking time.

Plaster mold for gorilla

Don't expect your first character to come out perfectly. If your first try is unsuccessful, cut the foam off the armature, and make another casting. Be careful measuring the formula. Your strong plaster mold should be able to make many copies of this character.

If you want a colored character, you can mix *casein paint* into the foam. It will end up darker after cooking. You can also paint the body after cooking, with a mixture of one-third latex paint to two-thirds liquid latex.

Liquid Foam Tools and Supplies

Tools

Hand-held electric mixer with separate bowl
Measuring spoons
Measuring cup
Masonite board
Rubber matting (*like that found on car floors*)
   Available at hardware stores
Kitchen oven

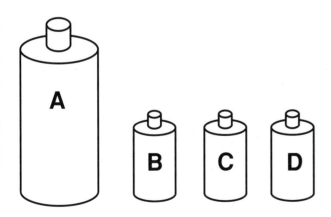

These four bottles contain the ingredients that make up the liquid foam rubber.

Supplies

Liquid foam rubber formula
   The Make-up Place
   1147 East Broadway
   Box 155
   Glendale, CA 90039
   Attn: Dennis Curcio
   (213) 669-1161
   Current price $43 per gallon (which will make a lot of characters), or $16 per quart.
   In winter, it must be shipped second-day air for $15 so it won't freeze. Dennis will send you a catalog of his supplies and costs for $1.
Mold release
   Also available from the Make-up Place. $4.25 per 8 ounces.
Ultra Cal 30
   Available at building supply houses. $26 per 100-pound package
Plasticine
$1/16''$ aluminum armature wire
$3/4''$ aluminum pushpins
Water-soluble clay
   Available from art supply houses
Crystal Clear spray
   Available from art supply houses
Petroleum jelly
   Available from pharmacies or supermarkets

9 Sets

Sky and Ground

Frequently, animators paint a large sheet of heavy white paper to look like sky, forest, or whatever is needed for their background.

For the basic *ground*, or floor, of the set they use a sheet of wood or Masonite clamped to a table. In clay animation, Plasticine covers this surface.

In foam rubber animation the wood or Masonite is covered with three or more layers of flat, corrugated cardboard or a three-inch-thick slab of very dense plastic foam or cork. This way, pushpins in the feet of the characters can stick in the surface.

If you stretch burlap over the cardboard and staple this to the wood ground, holes made by the pushpins will not be seen. You can decorate this material with acrylic paints and with sand. Hobby stores have a good selection of different colored sands, small pebbles, synthetic moss, and so on.

Buildings, Hills, and Mountains

You can make almost anything out of cut-down cardboard boxes. This will require a matte knife, a pencil, a pair of scissors, a ruler, and duct tape. Use a piece of *beaverboard* or corrugated cardboard for a cutting surface.

Take care when using a matte knife. Children under the age of twelve should be closely supervised, or an older person should do the cutting. Anyone using a matte knife for the first time should be shown how to use it.

Construct buildings and caves by cutting down cardboard boxes and holding the pieces together with duct tape. You can cover this with *papier-mâché* — a wonderful substance that you can use for almost anything. It is messy but safe.

To make papier-mâché, tear strips of newspaper and put them into a bucket containing water and wallpaper paste. After the strips have soaked for a while, take them out one at a time, and cover the surface of the cardboard with them.

Always tear, rather than cut, the strips. Smooth them onto the surface, and crisscross them for strength.

Apply two or more layers of papier-mâché. You could use newspaper for the first layer, and some other paper, such as torn-up grocery bags or white paper towels, for the second layer.

The different colors of the various kinds of paper will help you see when the first layer is completely covered by the second. Papier-mâché dries overnight, and is then ready to be painted.

Other substances you could use are *Paris Craft*, a gauze soaked with dry plaster; and *Theatremold* or *Mold Tex*, fluffy, powdery substances that you mix with water and apply like clay. All three dry very hard and are good for things such as buildings and mountaintops. Don't use them for areas of ground where characters walk, or you will have trouble making the pushpins penetrate.

Trees

The beginning set builder will probably find it difficult to make trees. One good trick is to go outside your house and gather some fallen twigs that look to be the right size for your trees. Stick one end of a twig into a tight hole in your set. You can form some brown Plasticine around the lower trunk and the ground to help the twig stand up. You can hang green hobby-shop foliage from the top branches.

Round wooden dowels, which are available from hardware stores, can also be used as tree trunks. You can wire cardboard branches to the dowels and coat them with brown Plasticine. Since Plasticine is heavy, use a thin coat.

Using papier-mâché or Theatremold to coat the tree and support the base of it is a stronger solution. Paint this brown when it dries.

Some students have simply cut a tree out of cardboard and taped a wooden dowel to the back of it. The dowel sticks out below the tree, so it can be inserted into the foam ground.

The insides of the trees on this page were made from Styrofoam cones. Small balls of green Plasticine were stuck on and slightly squashed to create branches. The assembly of the balls started at the bottom of the tree and worked around and upward.

Rocks

You can find real rocks for your set outside, or you could make fake ones. To do this, roll up balls of newspaper, cover them with papier-mâché, and paint them.

Another solution is to fasten the balls of newspaper roughly together with duct tape, cover them with Theatremold, and paint them when they are dry. You can also use cardboard cutouts painted to look like rocks and propped up from behind.

Our favorite technique is to tear up pieces of foam rubber, such as that found in mattresses. *Airbrush* with black, gray, and brown paint. If you do not have an airbrush, use a simple L-shaped ink-blowing tube found at art supply stores.

Do this project outside, where there is good ventilation, and where the sprayed ink won't mess up your house. These rocks look real when they are dry.

Grass

Fake grass from theater supply houses is usually too large or coarse for this kind of set. Instead, we buy bags of powdered grass from a hobby store. Spread a thin layer of white glue over the ground, and sprinkle the powder over it.

Shrubbery

You can purchase clumps of green foliage at hobby stores. Use this material for leaves, or bunch it together to form hedges. You can tear shrubbery and leafy sections of trees out of foam rubber and airbrush them. Some people make bushes from cutout cardboard stand-ups, which they paint on one side.

Ponds

If a pond has to hold real water, you must line it with Plasticine, and place the set in an area where spilled water will not hurt furniture or rugs. Most of the time it is best to avoid using real water. Instead, make your pond from blue Plasticine, or from cardboard painted blue.

Some people use mirrors. This is tricky because mirrors reflect whatever is directly above them. You will need to paint a sky and clouds on a sheet of cardboard and suspend it above the mirror, so the camera will see these reflected in the pond. If you don't have a mirror, you can lay a piece of glass on top of a piece of blue paper.

10 Special Effects for Three-dimensional Animation

How does a dragon fly? How does a puppet jump up and down? How do puppets throw a ball back and forth? How do you suspend anything in the air without the audience seeing the strings? How do you control the movement in the air?

Optical Illusion

The simplest way to throw a ball back and forth is to stick it to the background when it is not actually in the hands of the players. You do this by sighting very carefully through the camera lens. Position the ball on the background so it seems to be coming from the hands of the players. Use double-stick tape if the ball is lightweight. Plasticine balls can be stuck to a Plasticine wall.

If the ball is light enough and flat enough, fix a large sheet of clear plastic about one-quarter to one-half inch thick upright in the scene. Securely brace the plastic on all four sides, with the edges out of range of the camera. Fasten the ball to the plastic with double-stick tape. Take a few frames with the camera, and then move the ball slightly in the direction it is traveling.

Since the plastic is shiny, it may reflect a picture of the camera and operator, in addition to the scene being animated. Solve this problem by using a black shield.

Cut a small hole in the middle of a large sheet of black cardboard, so the camera lens can stick through it. Operate the camera from behind the cardboard. You will be able to see the scene only through the lens, while another person does the animation.

Appearing to be tossed through the air by his parents, the foam rubber baby opposite was actually fastened to a clear plastic sheet with double-stick tape.

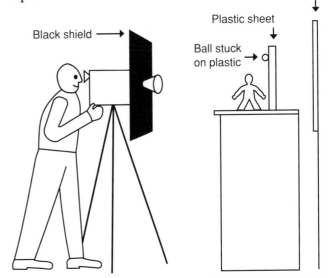

Black shield →

Background ↓

Plastic sheet ↓

Ball stuck on plastic →

Aerial Brace

The most common way to hold an object in midair is with an *aerial brace*. Attach clear fishing wire to the character in three spots. Fasten the other ends of the wires to something movable in the ceiling, such as a light boom or the construction described on pages 124 and 125. The character is braced in the air!

Braces can be simple, or they can have a lot of controls. To make a very simple brace, turn an eye screw into the ceiling and put a wire through the screw to raise or lower a ball. However, a ball having only one wire attached to it will spin. Using three wires prevents spinning.

You can create your own aerial brace out of whatever materials you have around the house. Remember that you must have something *above* the set to hold the suspended item. You must also be able to move things a little at a time, with a lot of control. Make things comfortable for yourself, as shots with aerial braces are very time-consuming. We do not recommend doing this in your first animation project!

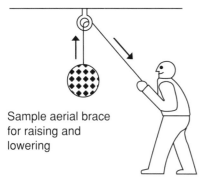

Sample aerial brace
for raising and
lowering

The aerial brace that worked best for us had a lot of controls. We made it from part of a tripod.

First, we fastened a triangular board to the tripod where the camera normally goes. Then, we removed the head and center post from the tripod and fastened them upside down to a block of wood nested on an overhead track. We flew all different kinds of characters using this setup.

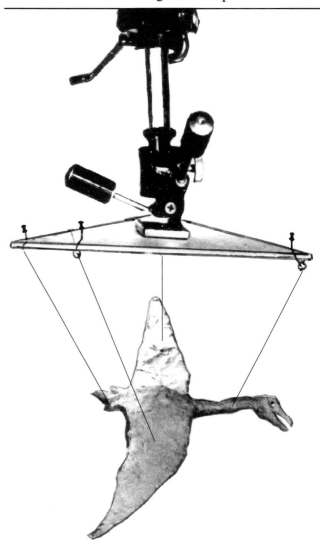

One of these was a flying dinosaur made out of Plasticine, with balsa wood and a wire armature inside the body. We attached clear fishing wire to four points on the body, including the two midwing sections, the upper neck, and the tail.

This pterodactyl had to be able to swoop down from a high position, flapping its wings, and pick someone up from the ground. That took a lot of different movements.

The tripod slid along the track to permit the forward and backward movements. Note the ruler along the edge of the track below.

Cranking the tripod up and down allowed the creature to swoop. The tilt and pan handles on the tripod moved the pterodactyl into different sloped positions.

The wings flapped when we repositioned the pushpins on top of the triangular board. Wires ran from the creature's body up through eyeholes under the triangle, looping over the pushpins.

When doing this kind of animation, look through the eyepiece of the camera to see if any light is reflected by the wires. If so, either change the position of your lights or paint the wires with permanent markers or acrylics to match the background.

Pixilation

Filming live people or everyday events one frame at a time is called *pixilation*.

In live-action filming, cameras run on batteries at the rate of twenty-four frames every second. A human operator would not be able to press the button for single-frame animation that fast.

If a camera were set up on a street to film a scene of traffic one frame at a time, the results would look like very fast moving traffic. A truck would be at one point in the first frame, then skip to a point much farther ahead in the next frame. Movement in between would have been missed.

If you had actors who could move through their paces slowly, you could even stop them for a moment to move some object in the scene. They would have to hold their positions while you were doing this.

An example of pixilation occurs in *Where Pizzas Crawl*. The film starts in a pizza parlor, with the cook tossing dough into the air.

Each time the dough comes down it's bigger. The cook makes a huge toss, and the pizza comes down in a playground. By this time it's huge, and it seems to be alive!

It chases a young girl across the playground. She jumps up to a horizontal pole to escape. The pizza gathers under her. She falls into it and is devoured. It closes over her, and lumps rise on its surface.

The next victims trip and fall while trying to escape. The pizza rises up, growing eyes, mouth, knife, and fork. After its lunch the pizza climbs a hill, burps, gets indigestion, and falls over a cliff.

The pizza was made out of a painted sheet with crumpled newspaper stapled under the edges for the crust.

The film *The Life of John Doe* has a lot of pixilation. During one scene in a park, a giant red dragon wraps its tongue around a boy, pulling him into its mouth.

We painted heavy white paper to look like a city park, and taped it to a wall. Then, we painted beaverboard to look like a sidewalk, and laid it on the floor.

We constructed a twelve-by-eight-foot dragon's head with a mouth that could be opened. We used a triple-thick corrugated cardboard called *Tri-Wall* to make the dragon.

We stapled this cardboard to a frame made of wood and chicken wire and covered it with Paris Craft. We used crumpled newspaper under the Paris Craft to make rounded areas.

Some of the scenes from this movie have already been described in the chapter on storyboards (page 88). The first scene that had to be pixilated was a long shot of the boy and dragon's head in the park. The red dragon opened its mouth, stuck out its long, green tongue (made of heavy paper), and dragged the screaming boy into its mouth.

The scene was shot four frames at a time. The boy held his position while someone ran into the scene to prop open the dragon's mouth with sticks of different lengths.

Each time the mouth opened a little wider, the tongue extended farther, finally wrapping around the boy and dragging him into the mouth.

Wooden frame for dragon's jaws

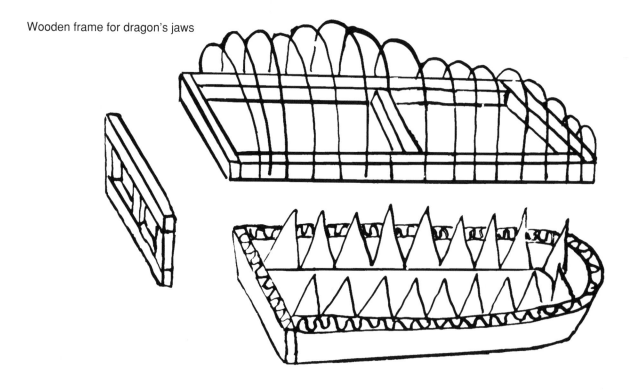

Filming *The Life of John Doe*. In the park, John Doe is
grabbed by the dragon's tongue.

This group project was made by twelve junior-high students. Each student made a sketch of a science-fiction scene that would be fun to work on. These were collected and given to four of the students, who chose the best ideas. Then, they drew up a storyboard.

While these four students were working, four others were rehearsed in make-up techniques. This included application of bald heads, fake noses, ears, beards, and mustaches. The remaining four shot a pixilated film on the make-up procedures.

Filming the scene in the mad scientists's laboratory

Each day, when the students arrived they would have new jobs — building sets or props, or making costumes. The next day they might operate the cameras or act in the film, shoot the animated sequences, or edit the footage that had come back from the lab. Everybody did every job, including work on the sound track.

The dragon floats in the water of an underground
cave. John Doe, who has just climbed out of
the dragon's jaws, exclaims, "That was quite an
experience!"

Matte Box

We used a *matte box* several times when making *The Life of John Doe*. We wanted to have our huge dragon's head open its mouth to eject our hero. The dragon had to float on water in an underground cave. We could paint a paper background for the cave, but how could we use real water?

We solved the problem inexpensively by filming the dragon through a matte box. A matte box is a picture frame attached to the front of the camera. This frame has a sheet of glass or clear plastic in it.

You place a piece of thin black cardboard called a *matte* in this frame to hide the part of the scene that you don't want to film.

In the case of *John Doe*, we filmed the whole scene through a matte box, with the bottom third of the scene hidden. The matte covered the area just below the dragon's lower jaw, where the water was going to be.

Exposure 1

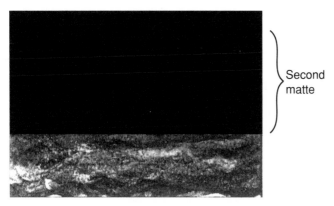

Exposure 2

The result

Then, we covered the lens, and *backwound* the film to the place where we had started shooting. At this time we changed the matte.

Then, we placed a piece of black cardboard in the top two-thirds of the matte box, with its edge just touching the top of the first matte. Then, we removed the first matte and uncovered the lens.

While the actor went to lunch, we pointed the camera at a piece of cardboard that had been painted blue. All the lens could see was the blue color in the bottom third of the scene. To distort the image, we held ripple glass in front of the lens and moved the glass as the scene was shot.

The result was a huge dragon's head floating in rippling blue water in an underground cave. You can buy or build matte boxes for super-8mm and 16mm cameras, but you must be able to backwind the film in the camera so you can make two exposures on the same piece of film.

This is easy to do with a Bolex camera, but not all super-8mm cameras can do this. Separate *back-winders* for super-8mm film can be purchased.

In video, matting is accomplished using the *chroma key* technique. One camera films a person in front of a blue screen. A second camera films something else, such as a city scene.

As the elements are combined into one image during filming, the blue area filmed by the first camera is rejected. The combined image shows the person in front of the scene filmed by the second camera.

11   Computer Animation

Macintosh 512

Besides using cameras for animating, you can also use computers.

Advantages

Computer animation doesn't require the purchase of art supplies. The work area is clean — no paint or clay on the floor, no cleanup of spills. You don't need storage space for big sets.

If you already have a Macintosh or an Amiga computer at home, this technique would be inexpensive. You don't have to purchase or develop film. Computer disks are cheaper than film stock.

You don't have to wait for results because computers have instant playback. You can copy the animation to video if you have an Amiga computer.

Computers are laborsaving for some types of animation because, after you have created the animation, you can test out changes or modifications without destroying the original artwork.

Amiga 2000

Disadvantages

Computer equipment is more expensive than super-8mm film equipment, but costs about as much as 16mm or video equipment.

With computers, you don't get the physical contact with art supplies that many animators enjoy. Some artists prefer the feeling of drawing with pencils, painting with brushes, and modeling with clay.

The original artwork for some types of animation can take longer to prepare on a computer than in other ways.

Finished computer animation is shown on a computer monitor, which has a small screen. If you have an Amiga and a VCR, the animation can be copied to videotape and shown on a TV screen or a large video-projection screen. Copying computer animation to film for large-screen projection can be expensive.

You make drawings on a computer by pressing a button on the mouse and moving it around on your table, which feels very different from sketching with a pencil. The drawings appear on the screen of the monitor as you make them.

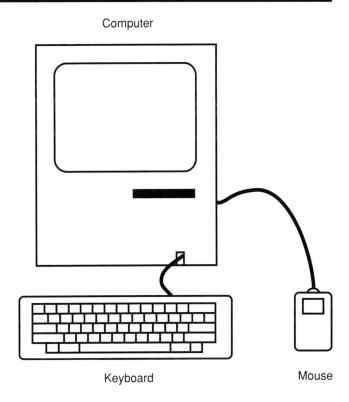

Computer

Keyboard   Mouse

The Macintosh Computer

Turn on the computer and insert a *program disk* in the *floppy disk drive* of the computer. A program disk looks like a flat, square piece of plastic with a hole in the middle, but it has information inside. When you put the disk in the drive, you have loaded the computer with some specific "tools."

Each program is different and lets you do different things. The *MacWrite* program for the Macintosh lets you write letters and papers. The *MacPaint* program lets you make drawings.

In addition to inserting a program disk into the computer, you must also insert a blank disk into the extra disk drive on which to record your letters or drawings.

A blank disk acts like a tablet of paper. It has many "pages" available for you to "write" on. Computer people think of blank disks as filing cabinets, and of all the separate writings or drawings you would normally do on paper instead appear on the screen as *files* in the cabinet.

When learning to use a computer, first read the computer manual for specific instructions.

The first time you insert a blank disk into the Macintosh disk drive, you need to *initialize* it. This means you get it ready to receive information and you give it a name.

It's a good idea to keep the same sorts of information or drawings together. If you were going to do a series of drawings about animals and another series about cars in the city, you might initialize one disk and call it "Animals," and initialize the other disk and call it "Cars."

Macintosh computer

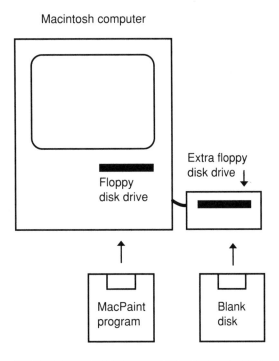

Floppy
disk drive

Extra floppy
disk drive ↓

MacPaint
program

Blank
disk

Name each page, or *file*, on your disk. Suppose you make a drawing of a white car driving down a dark city street. After you finish making the drawing, *save* the drawing onto your "Cars" disk, and title it "White Car." Eject the disk, and turn off the computer.

Later, when you want to see the drawing on the computer screen again, insert the disk into the computer. Use the mouse to display the titles of all your files on the screen. Choose the title "White Car" with the mouse, and the drawing will reappear. Then, you can make changes in it if you wish.

After you have finished your drawings each day, make a copy, or backup, of the drawing on a spare disk, in case the original disk gets damaged.

If you have a Macintosh computer, practice making drawings using the MacPaint and *MacDraw* programs.

A *printer* is a useful piece of equipment. After you have made a drawing, you can signal the printer to copy it onto paper. If you don't have a printer, you can only see the images on the computer screen.

These black-and-white printed images can be painted and filmed like flip books.

There are several types of Macintosh computers currently available — the 512K, 512K Enhanced, Mac Plus, Macintosh SE, and Macintosh 2. All of these work with a black-and-white monitor except the Macintosh 2, which uses color.

These are listed in order of cost and amount of *memory*. Having more memory makes animation easier by allowing better movements and more detailed drawings.

If you have a 512K, which is one of the older models, you can take it to a service center to be *enhanced*. Then, it will take *double-sided disks*, which are more useful for computer animation.

After you have become familiar with the MacPaint program and can use all the tools, consider the animation programs available for the Macintosh.

Macintosh Animation Programs

We have used the *Video Works* program. This program lets you make a series of drawings and run the drawings on the screen in sequence like a movie.

Video Works also has a sound component. After you have drawn and edited your scenes, you can add sounds to them. You have your choice of a few pieces of classical, jazz, and rock music, along with many different sound effects.

The computer will run your picture and sound at the same time. You can edit your sound, changing where it starts in the film.

Some artists have found the *Hyper Animator* program useful. It is used by museums, galleries, and artists who want to make a series of short scenes with which the viewer can interact.

Computer   Printer

Digitizer

A fun accessory for your computer is the *digitizer*. This setup requires a small TV camera. You might be able to use the video camera you already have, or you can buy a cheap black-and-white surveillance camera like those used in banks.

In addition to the digitizer, which is a small box that connects to the back of your computer, you will need some lights. The digitizer for the Macintosh comes with its own program disk, which is called *MacVision*.

If you use a surveillance camera, you will find it useful to have a small video monitor. This will show your image on the screen more quickly and let you make the printing modifications much faster than if you had to wait for the image to show up on the computer screen.

The digitizer is meant to be used with still images. If the person posing for the snapshot moves, an interesting distortion will occur.

With this setup you can tape your own face or still pictures from magazines. It's also possible to digitize still shots from live-action videos you have already shot.

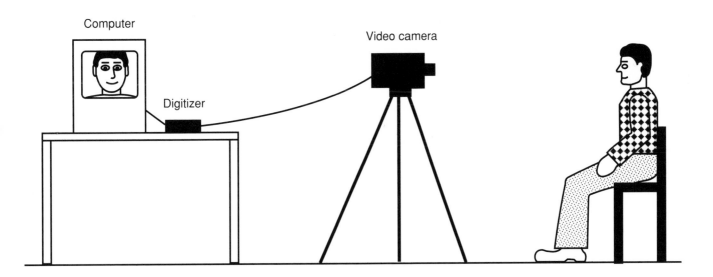

We did this with our Sony Video 8 Pro CCD-V220 camcorder connected to the digitizer.

Once these images are in the computer, you can change them. For instance, you could draw a mustache on your face or draw a new background for yourself.

Then, you can insert these digitized images into the Video Works program and animate them.

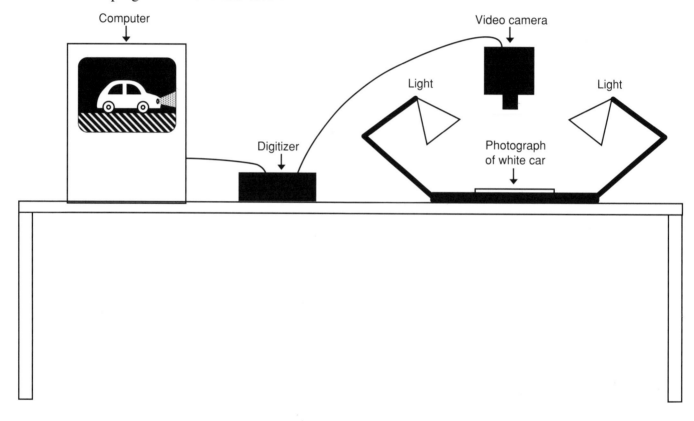

The Amiga 2000

The *Amiga 2000* is a popular computer at art schools and with independent animators. This machine was first made for video games, so it was programmed to interface with video equipment.

A color computer in the same general price range as the Macintosh, the Amiga has good programs for animation, graphics, tilting, and interaction with live-action video.

As with the Macintosh, besides the actual Amiga computer, you will also need a monitor, a keyboard, and a mouse. The disk drive for the main program of the Amiga is inside the computer, and you can also have the second disk drive (highly desirable) installed inside the computer instead of outside.

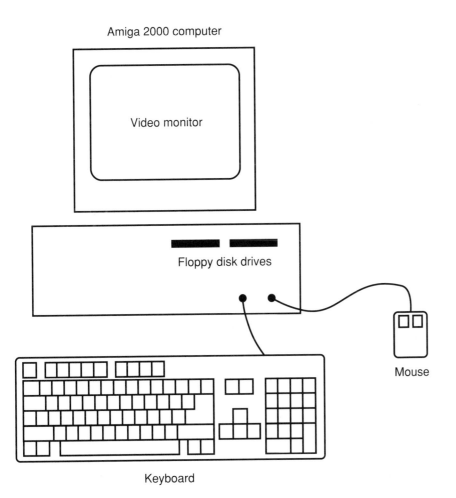

Amiga 2000 computer

Video monitor

Floppy disk drives

Mouse

Keyboard

Amiga Animation Programs

The computer comes with a basic program, which is called *Workbench*. After you have familiarized yourself with this program, you can learn *Deluxe Paint*, which is a general draw-and-paint program with four thousand colors.

Once these basics are mastered, you can try two animation programs that we have used. *Page Flipper* is a very simple program. It lets you stack up your drawings so they can be run one right after another, as in an animated film. This is a good program for a beginner.

Zoetrope has a variety of possibilities, but not too much complexity. It lets you see your previous drawing in pale blue under the new drawing you are making. This helps you to make the proper changes for animation. It can also quickly run the last group of drawings you have made, so you can see how the animation looks.

With the Amiga and an accessory called Genlock, you can make titles on top of live-action video images. You can also do many special effects that combine live-action video and animation.

We have noticed that operating a computer is like learning to ride a bike. You must practice the various functions until they become second nature. Once you are well rehearsed with a tool, it becomes a wonderful creative instrument, and you can be freer about creating art, perhaps creating some things that you could never have made without a computer.

Filmmaking equipment and technology have been around for a long time, without many changes. We have only had video for a short time, and there have already been more changes and improvements. Computer animation is new and is still undergoing rapid change. We expect both video and computer equipment to become less expensive, easier to operate, and more useful to home animators.

12   Editing

Editing is fun and easy. It is somewhat like assembling photos in a scrapbook in a certain order to tell a certain story. Some people find it the most fun part of filmmaking. Sometimes, you can completely change the meaning of a film just by how you edit it.

It is not always convenient to shoot your scenes in the same order you want them to appear in the finished film or videotape. Use editing:

- to assemble scenes in the final order.
- to remove mistakes.
- to shorten scenes.
- to divide scenes for placement in different parts of the film.
- to synchronize the sound track with the picture.

Editing scenes in super 8mm

Editing in Super 8mm

Screen your new film on a projector before editing. Super-8mm *editors* (editing machines) do not run at exactly eighteen or twenty-four frames per second. However, projectors will run the film at the proper speed, so you can see if a scene is too slow or too fast.

Cut apart the scenes and hang them from an *editing rack*. If you don't have a rack, tape the *head,* or beginning, of each scene to the edge of your table, and drop the *tail*, or end, of each scene into a clean paper bag.

It is important to keep the film clean. Even a small piece of dust on film can cause a scratch. Wipe off the worktable or cover the area with white paper. Wash your hands. See page 148 for instructions on how to clean film.

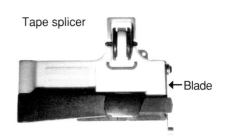

Tape splicer

Blade

Before splicing your actual movie, practice on scrap film and white leader. We use the Guillotine super-8mm *tape splicer*.

Open the flap of the splicer and place scrap film in the groove so it extends past the edge of the splicer. The pins of the splicer should stick up through the perforations in the film.

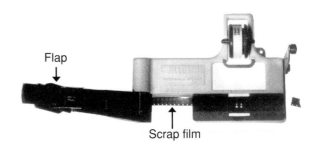

Flap

Scrap film

Bring the blade down so that it cuts off the edge of the film. Take the film off, and do the same thing with a piece of white leader.

Place the film and the leader in the groove of the splicer so that the two freshly cut ends meet in the center.

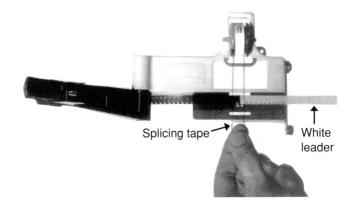

Splicing tape

White leader

Draw the splicing tape down across the place where the film and leader meet. Smooth the tape down with your finger.

Close the flap, and press it down. This will punch perforations in the tape to match those in the film. It will also cut off the tape.

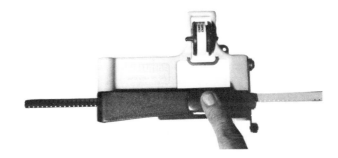

Pick up the right end of the film with your right hand. Peel the spliced film off the splicer.

There will be a small extra piece of tape sticking out past the edge of the film.

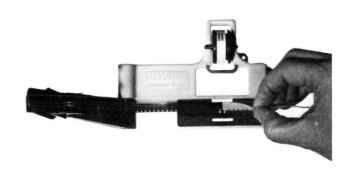

Hold the film near the splice with your left hand. With the index finger of your right hand, fold the extra tape *very tightly* over the other side of the film. Be sure no edge of tape sticks out.

Splices must be perfect, or the projector may tear up your film!

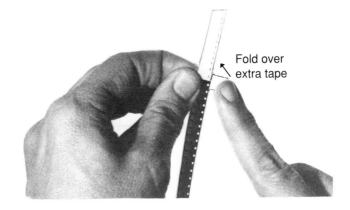

Fold over extra tape

Splice six feet of super-8mm white leader onto the head of your film. You will use this to thread the projector. Next come the titles; then your film scenes; then the end titles. At the tail, splice on three feet of white leader.

On most super-8mm viewers, the film winds over the top of the feed reel, through the viewer, and over the top of the take-up reel. The edge of the film with the perforations is closest to you.

After editing, rewind the film back onto your take-up reel, leaving the head facing out. Remove the film from the editor. Then, you can project it.

If the film got dirty during editing, clean it before you project it by winding it through a pad of Vebril Wipes or some white velvet cloth.

If the film is very dirty, moisten the cloth with liquid movie cleaner first. Rewind it slowly so that the liquid has time to dry before the film is rewound.

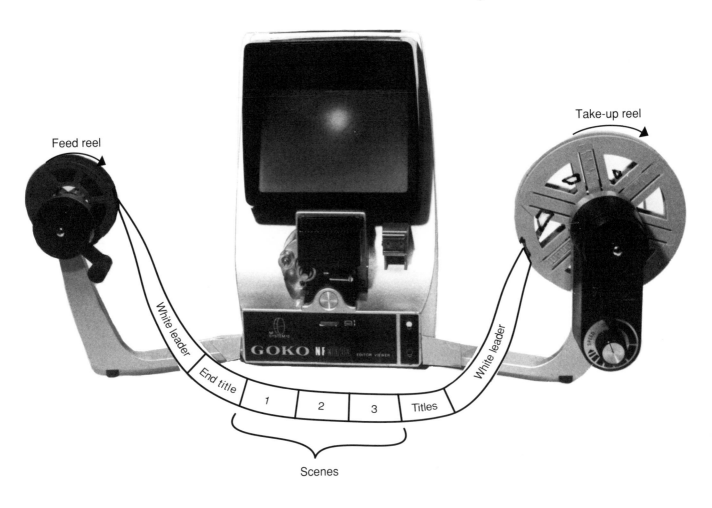

Below, some students are using a fancy super-8mm editing table to synchronize super-8mm pictures with separate super-8mm *full-coat sound track*. The separate sound track is the same size as super-8mm film, with the same perforations.

Editing in 16mm

You need a 16mm viewer, a set of *rewinds*, and a 16mm tape splicer to edit 16mm film. These can be rented for a day if you don't want to own them. The procedures are almost exactly the same for 16mm as for super 8mm.

Screen your footage in a 16mm movie projector. You can rent one, or you might be able to use the projector at school. Some public libraries lend them to responsible borrowers.

Clean your work area and your hands. If you have shot negative film, do not open that package. Edit only the copy, or *work print*. If your film needs a lot of editing, cut your scenes apart and hang them up on a rack or from the edge of the table into paper bags.

Practice making five perfect splices with scrap 16mm film or black leader. Then assemble your film, editing scenes from right to left, from head to tail. Wind the film toward the right and *under* the rewinds as you progress.

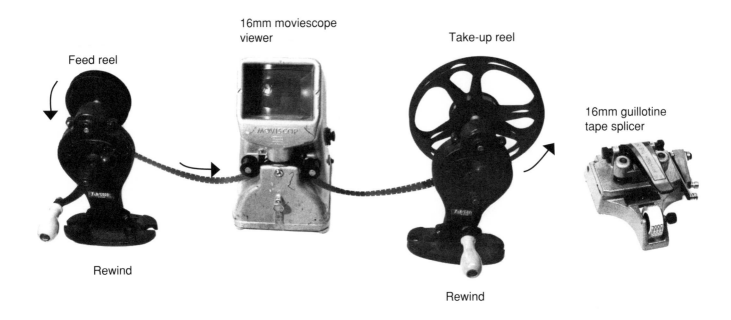

Feed reel

16mm moviescope viewer

Take-up reel

16mm guillotine tape splicer

Rewind

Rewind

16mm film has *edge numbers*. Be sure they are on the top edge (farther away from you), and are readable as in the diagram below. This confirms that the film is in the right position, and is not being edited upside down and backward.

If you are editing a work print, and want to splice together two scenes, cut off and discard the last frame of the first scene and the first frame of the second scene.

This is necessary because the original negative (which you will not touch) will have to be *hot spliced* at a lab if you want to make copies from it. A hot splicer uses up more frames than does a tape splicer.

When you have finished editing, clean the film and rewind it back onto its take-up reel, heads out, so it will be ready to project.

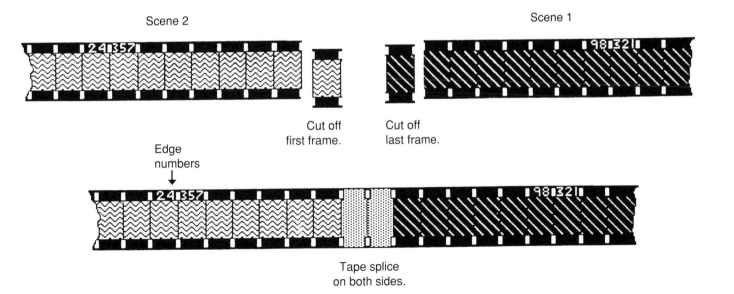

Scene 2

Scene 1

Cut off first frame.

Cut off last frame.

Edge numbers

Tape splice on both sides.

Video Editing

Video editing is very different from film editing. In film editing you touch the actual film, cut it, and splice scenes into different positions. In video editing, you never actually touch the tape. You do not cut or splice it.

Instead, you locate the scenes you want to use and copy them onto a clean tape in the order you want them.

Try to make decisions ahead of time, because it is more difficult to shorten and lengthen scenes, or to change their position after you have finished copying them. Going back and making a change means you will have to do a new edit of the whole video piece — unless you have access to expensive equipment.

You will need two TVs or monitors, two VCRs, and a central *editing controller*. Insert the videotape with the original picture and sound into the *player* side of your setup. Insert a blank videocassette into the *recorder* side.

If you have decided to use scenes 1, 4, 7, and 10 from your original tape, you must copy them in the order you want onto the recorder side of the setup. Pressing the correct buttons on the editing controller causes it to give directions to the two VCRs.

Always try to shoot extra footage at the head and tail of each scene when you shoot videotape. VCRs need about five seconds extra to get up to speed for smooth editing.

Smooth editing means there are no glitches or "snow" seen between scenes. Your VCR must have a *flying erase head* in order to do this.

If you do not have a complete video-8 editing setup, you can use your Sony Video 8 Pro CCD-V220 camcorder instead of the player VCR and its eyepiece viewer instead of one monitor. Then, you need only one half-inch VCR and one TV or monitor. This way, you copy video-8 material onto the half-inch tape. Sony makes a special video editing controller for this setup.

If you have access to ½- or ¾-inch video editing equipment, you can copy and edit your video-8 tape into those formats. When you finish editing, you then copy it back to video-8 or half-inch tape.

We recommend these procedures only for normal *scene-to-scene* editing, not for *frame-by-frame* editing, because only the more expensive editing equipment allows you control over single frames.

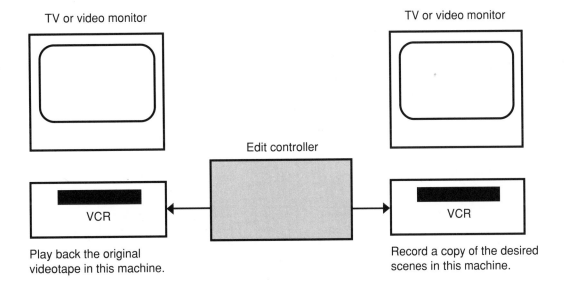

TV or video monitor

TV or video monitor

Edit controller

VCR

VCR

Play back the original
videotape in this machine.

Record a copy of the desired
scenes in this machine.

13 Sound Tracks

Part of the effect of your film comes from the pictures. The other part comes from the *sound track*. You can make a simple sound track by playing music on a record player or cassette deck at the same time you show your film or videotape. If you use this method, look for music with the right atmosphere.

Music

Most pieces of popular music are about three minutes long. Most classical music is longer. Your first animated film may be from twenty seconds to one minute long, so you will need a segment of music that is close to the right length. Music is made up of phrases — short segments of sound, like the phrases in a sentence.

You may choose music that starts in the middle of a record. For this reason, it's good to isolate the musical phrase or passage you will use by taping it onto quarter-inch (open-reel) audiotape or onto an audiocassette.

If you are working with quarter-inch audiotape, splice in white quarter-inch sound tape leader at the beginning and end. For audiocassettes, zero the counter on the cassette deck just before the start of the sound you plan to use.

If you use music created and performed by other people, you may show your film to friends and relatives, or in a nonprofessional situation without getting permission from the people who own the rights to the music. Television airings and theatrical showings require written permission.

A more exciting idea is to make the music yourself or to have your friends do it. You can gather four to six people in a room with an assortment of drumming instruments such as toys, pots and pans, sticks, and wastepaper baskets. Instruments designed by Carl Orff, which can be found in elementary schools, are also excellent for making your own music.

Each person chooses an instrument. The first person makes four sounds and repeats them over and over without changing them. As soon as this sound is going well, the next person adds four repeated sounds. When the two of them are synchronized, the third and then the fourth person adds in four sounds. Once everybody is playing, you can make a recording.

You can play back this recording with the picture. After making a few sound tracks, try recording the players making their sounds while watching the film. Later, you can choose which sound track you like the best.

You can also make original music on a *synthesizer*. Some inexpensive ones let you make notes that sound like different instruments. Some of your friends may have their own bands and create original music. After your film or videotape is finished, you can have them come to your house with their instruments to make the sound track while watching your film.

Voices

Some very good films don't have any music. They have sound effects or voices. If you refer to the chapter on stories and storyboards, you will find that the first film, *In the Middle* (page 84), only has a voice telling a story and making some sound effects.

Professionally, voices for an animated film are recorded first, and the animation is done to match the voices.

If you wanted to make the sound track ahead of time, you could use the technique described opposite. For this, you divide words into syllables and make mouths in three different sizes. These make the character look as if he is talking — opening and closing his mouth on each syllable.

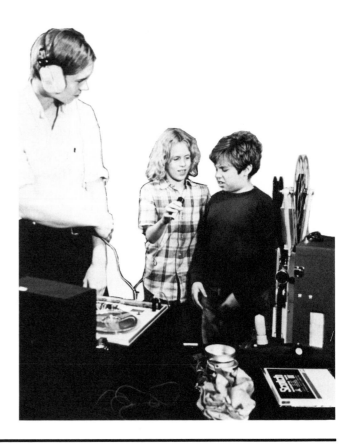

Some animators speak words while watching them-selves in a mirror. They draw different shaped mouths for different syllables.

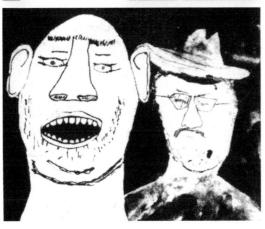

At the Yellow Ball Workshop, if we film a char-acter in the distance and he has a small face, we consider *lip synch* (synchronizing the mouth with the sound) unnecessary. When filming the close-ups, we try to have the character speak only one or two sentences. We make a diagram of the number of times the mouth must open and close for each syllable, and animate it according to that diagram.

Mouth opens

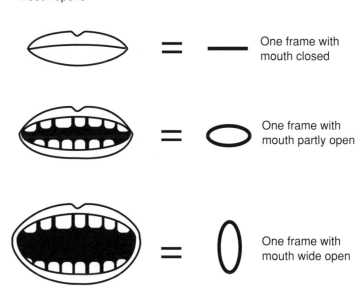

= —— One frame with mouth closed

= ⬭ One frame with mouth partly open

= ⬯ One frame with mouth wide open

Diagram for talking

− − ○ O ○ − ○ O ○ − −

Hi,   there.

Sound Effects

Records with sound effects are available, but most of the time you can make the effects yourself, including cats, dogs, traffic, babies crying, wind, fire, rain, explosions, doors slamming, fistfights, gunshots, horses galloping, doors creaking, screams, restaurant sounds, and so on.

It is technically easier to try to make the sounds yourself or with your friends while watching the movie. If you need a lot of different sounds, you can divide the work among several people. Give each person a specific job to do at a specific time. One can do the creaking door, and a little later, the scream. Another can do the footsteps and the wind. You can run the projector while someone else records the sound track.

Show your friends the film first. Then, rehearse each of them to see who does which sound best. After that, try making the sounds with the movie running. You will have to do this a few times before everyone comes in exactly on cue.

Using this technique means you don't have to cut, edit, and splice the sound track. It will save you a lot of time. If you only have an audiocassette recorder, use this method, because it is better not to splice audiocassette tape.

Editing Sound

Quarter-inch *reel-to-reel* tape recorders are more flexible for editing. For instance, you can record many sounds of creaking doors, and splice in the one you like best.

If you are going to edit sound tracks, get a copy of your film made first. You will project this copy many times during editing, and it will get scratched. This way, you can save the clean print for performances.

You can cut and splice sound tracks together as with film. The main difference is that you put the splicing tape only on one side. We use an Edit-All quarter-inch sound tape splicer.

Edit-All quarter-inch
sound tape splicer

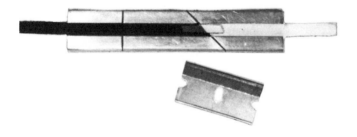

Mixing Sound

Suppose that after you get all these sounds edited and synchronized with your picture, the track seems a little empty. You might like to add music on top of the effects and voices.

With a *sound-on-sound* reel-to-reel quarter-inch tape deck, you can record all your voices and effects on one track and then edit them. Then, you can go back and record a music track onto the other track of the tape.

Some super-8mm projectors allow you to record two different sound tracks onto striped super-8mm film.

If you are working in 16mm, you will need a two- or four-track quarter-inch tape recorder to get all your tracks onto the same tape. Otherwise, you can play back your tracks on two tape decks at the same time, recording them on a single tape in a third deck.

Professional animators make completely separate sound tracks for each element — music, effects, and voices. Every person who speaks often has his own separate voice track. Most of the effects have separate tracks, and the music is on a separate track. Sometimes, there are sixteen or more different tracks.

The sound engineer records each of these sounds on quarter-inch audiotape, and then copies this to a 16mm track. This *full coat* is the same size as 16mm film and has the same perforations along one side.

Editors synchronize the film and the sound on an editing table called a *Steenbeck*. Then, they take the tracks to a sound studio and *mix* them down onto one track.

A professional sound mix is mainly used to raise or lower the volumes of the different sounds in relationship to each other.

Sounds on tape can be separated and spliced together
the same way the film (picture) is edited.

How to Get the Sound onto Your Film or Videotape

You can always run your picture with a separate sound track, but suppose you want the sound *on* the film or videotape itself and always perfectly synchronized?

Super 8mm

After editing your super-8mm film, send it off to get a *sound-striped* copy made. Project this copy on a super-8mm sound projector and record the sounds live, directly into the microphone of the projector.

If you have a more elaborate sound track, make it on another tape recorder first. Then, attach the projector and the tape deck with a *patch cord*, and record the sound onto the sound-striped film. If you have a sound camera, you can use sound-striped film from the start.

16mm Film

After editing your film, make your sound track on a separate audiocassette or quarter-inch tape deck. Get it to the point where you can run it in synchronization with the picture. You can do this if the film is not more than three minutes long. At this point, if you don't have access to sound studios or editing tables, give the picture and track to a film lab, and ask them to make you a print with an *optical sound track* on it. Give them a *synch sheet,* which is a listing of the scenes and the sound that accompany them. Optical sound tracks can be expensive, so check prices!

Videotape

After editing your animated scenes, make a separate sound track on an audiocassette or quarter-inch tape deck. Run a patch cord between the *output* of the audiotape deck and the *audio input* of a VCR, which you will use as a *recorder*.

Load your silent, edited video animation into a second VCR, which you will use as a *player*. Run a patch cord from its *video output* to the *video input* of the *recorder* VCR. Record the picture and the sound at the same time onto the *recorder* VCR.

If your VCR has an *audio dub* function, you can watch your silent video and record, or dub, a sound track onto it at the same time, without erasing the video.

Appendix

Students and Their Work

Most of the work shown in this book was created over a period of twenty-five years at the Yellow Ball Workshop in Lexington, Massachusetts, and fifteen years at the Newton Creative Art Center, in Newton, Massachusetts.

Thousands of wonderful students participated. Some met briefly in workshops in other cities, states, and countries, and some attended the Yellow Ball Workshop for many years.

We hired assistant instructors from the ranks of former students. These assistants ranged in age from fourteen to nineteen years old. Those who did this job at some time in their career at the Yellow Ball Workshop are identified with an (a) after their name even if they were not assistants at the time represented by the pictures shown.

Group Projects

The Life of John Doe,
pages 129, 130, 132
Michael Wilson, Chris Tait, Tom Hacsunda, Jeffrey Bowman, David Feld, Daniel Kontoff, Marc Bischoff, Steven Goldblatt, Marty Ekman, Jon Feld, James Robinson, Kenny Prop, Paul Falcone (ages 12–15).

The Golden Ball,
pages 102, 103, 122
Julia Antonian, Arevik Mandrikian, Anush Mikayelian, Sara Stine, Tigran Mikayelian, Michael Shahinjian, Miran Shahinjian, Jeremy Woodruff, Greg Horwitch, Carl Huebner, Andy Presby, Ann Quinney (ages 11–15)

A Drop of Honey,
pages 52, 56, 82
Ann Quinney, Jeremy Woodruff, Greg Horwitch, Tigran Mikayelian, Peter Fohl, Aram Demirjian, Arek Bayandour, Ahmed Cook (ages 11–13).

Where Pizzas Crawl,
pages 126, 127
Eric Brown, Rosemary Fabian, Sarah Kirshner, Alan Berkowitz, Mary Callahan (ages 12–15).

The Cosmic Crystal by Paul Falcone,
page 14
ACTORS: Jan Drury (pictured), Steve Ria, Joel Light, Jean Falcone, Andrea Casson, Paul Falcone (age 14).

Photographs and Technical Drawings

by Yvonne Andersen

Other Artwork and Scenes

Equipment and Film Sources and Services

These are fast-moving times. Stores stop selling some products and start selling others. Film labs change their services. If you can't find appropriate services, equipment, and supplies in your part of the country, here are some places we use.

Labs for Developing Film

Cine Service Lab
1380 Soldiers Field Rd.
Brighton, MA 02135
(617) 862-4283
(16mm film)

Film Tech, Inc.
181 Notre Dame St.
Westfield, MA 01085
(413) 568-8605
(16mm film/prints)

Film Service Lab
93 Harvey St.
Cambridge, MA 02140
(617) 547-8501
(super-8mm b&w film)

Kodalux
925 Page Mill Rd.
Palo Alto, CA 94304
Customer Service: Dixie Matthews
(415) 494-7555
(8mm & super-8mm color film)

Film Stock and Leader

Camera stores, drugstores, labs or:
Eastman Kodak, New York, NY
Call (800) 634-6101 to order
16mm film, super-8mm b&w film,
or catalog of film stock and leader.
Call (800) 462-4676 to order
super-8mm color film stock.

Video and Super-8mm Film Equipment

Super 8 Sound
95 Harvey St.
Cambridge, MA 02140
(617) 876-5876

Eclipse Film/Video
95 Harvey St.
Cambridge, MA 02140
(617) 491-4433

Newtonville Camera
249 Walnut St.
Newtonville, MA 02160
(617) 965-1240

16mm Film/Video Equipment

Crimson Camera Technical
325 Vassar St.
Cambridge, MA 02139
(617) 868-5150

Adler's Photo Store
62–66 Orange St.
Providence, RI 02903
(401) 331-7320

Video Animation Stand
Animation Controls, Inc.
1040 Joshua Way
Vista, CA 92083
(619) 598-2146

Optical Printers

Meritex, Inc. (formerly J. K. Camera Engineering)
5101 San Leandro St.
Oakland, CA 94601
(415) 534-9018

Used Equipment

Chambless Productions
2488 Jewel St.
Atlanta, GA 30344
(404) 767-5210
(super 8mm/16mm)

International Center for 8mm Film & Video
10-R Oxford St.
Somerville, MA 02143
Attn: Toni Treadway
(617) 666-3372

Computer Hardware and Software

Ferranti Dege Two (Macintosh)
455 Brookline Ave.
Boston, MA 02215
(617) 232-2550

Memory Locations (Amiga)
396 Washington St.
Wellesley, MA 02181
(617) 237-6846

Mac Connections (Macintosh)
14 Mill St.
Marlow, NH 03456
(800) 622-5472

Super-8mm to Video Transfer

Brodsky and Treadway
10-R Oxford St.
Somerville, MA 02143
(617) 666-3372
(transfer to broadcast video)

Art Supply Sources

Drawing on Film

Special supplies listed on page 17.

Flip Books

4″ × 6″ white scratch pads, markers, and pens from stationery stores. Field guides, peg bars, light boxes from animation supply houses.

Cutouts

Medium-finish 2-ply bristol board, markers, brushes, inks, paints, tape, scissors from art supply stores.

Effects

Animation cels, cel paint, peg bars, rolls of acetate for snow and rain, other animation supplies from
Cartoon Colour Company
9024 Lindblade Ave.
Culver City, CA 90232-2584
(213) 838-8467

Nonglare picture glass, ground glass, mirrors (including front-surface mirrors with silver coating on front instead of back, which gives a better image), ripple glass (Blenko) from glass supply stores.

Clay Animation

Plasticine from art supply stores.

Xerography

Most towns have photocopying centers where your pictures can be duplicated, made larger or smaller, or made darker or lighter.

Microfiche machines for copying film onto printing-out paper from super-8mm or 16mm film frames can be found at some libraries.

Puppet Animation

Aluminum armature wire, long-shank pushpins, foam core, corrugated cardboard, acrylic paints from art supply stores.

Styrofoam, thread, double-stick tape, matte knives, map tacks, beads, burlap, Paris Craft from arts-and-crafts stores.

Cut foam rubber from foam rubber stores that sell pillows and mattresses.

Colored sands, small pebbles, moss, fake shrubbery, balsa wood from hobby shops.

Wood, Masonite, C clamps from lumberyards or hardware stores.

Liquid Foam Rubber Characters

Special supplies listed on page 115.

Animation Magazine

This is the only magazine on the subject which is directed at both the general public and the animation industry. It is published by the people who present the *Los Angeles International Animation Celebration* and the traveling *International Tournee of Animation*, which appears at movie houses across the country. Subscriptions: *Animation* Magazine, 6750 Centinela Ave., Suite 300, Culver City, CA 90230; (213) 313-9214.

ASIFA (Association Internationale du Film d' Animation)

This is the international association for animators. Members get free admission to screenings, invitations to special events at all ASIFA-sponsored animation festivals, and a subscription to *ASIFA News*, a quarterly international publication. They also receive local newsletters, which include information about film showings and international film festivals, including those for children. This is an important organization to join. For membership in your area, contact:

ASIFA-East
c/o The Optical House
111 Eighth Ave., Room 914
New York, NY 10011
(212) 869-5840

ASIFA-Central
c/o Dave Darushka
790 N. Milwaukee Ave.
Chicago, IL 60622
(312) 266-4300

ASIFA-Washington
PO Box 53101
Washington, DC 20009

ASIFA-Northwest
c/o Marilyn Zornado
5804 N.E. Freemont St.
Portland, OR 97213
(503) 225-1130
Pres. Joanna Priestly

ASIFA-San Francisco
c/o Karl Cohen
PO Box 14516
San Francisco, CA 94114
(415) 386-1004

ASIFA-Hollywood
PO Box 787
Burbank, CA 91503
(818) 508-5224

Animated Films and Videotapes

Twenty-six reels of award-winning animated films made by children can be rented or purchased in 16mm color sound prints from the Yellow Ball Workshop, 62 Tarbell Ave., Lexington, MA 02173; (617) 862-4283.

The International Tournee of Animation may be purchased on videotape from *Animation,* PO Box 25547, Los Angeles, CA 90025, Attn: Videos.

Masters of Animation, a collection of four videotapes assembled by John Halas, includes excerpts from some of the best international animation. It is available from Home Vision, 5547 N. Ravenswood Ave., Chicago, IL 60640-1199. The book *Masters of Animation* is published by Salem House Publishers, 462 Boston St., Topsfield, MA 01983.

Animated films and videos can sometimes be borrowed from public libraries if booked in advance. Some of the more popular titles can be rented from local video rental houses. There are many commercial film distributors that rent and sell some animated films in super 8mm, 16mm, and half-inch video.

For some of the famous animated films made in association with the National Film Board of Canada contact Karol Media, Riverside Dr., Wayne, NJ 07470-3190; (201) 628-9111.

Index

Italic page numbers refer to illustrations.